To Jem a[...]
much [...]
very happy Christmas

Lys
and Kevin xxxx

The honey·ant men's love song

R.M.W. (Bob) Dixon, Professor of Linguistics at the Australian National University, has taught at Harvard University and was a Fulbright Fellow at the University of California, Santa Cruz. He has written grammars of four Australian languages from North Queensland and studied the kinship system and the language of songs. He has also published a general survey volume, *The Languages of Australia* (Cambridge University Press, 1980).

Martin Duwell was born in England and has lived in Australia since 1957. He is a lecturer in the English Department of the University of Queensland where he teaches Rhetoric, Australian Literature and Old Icelandic. He was for many years the owner and editor of the poetry publisher Makar Press and later was poetry editor for the University of Queensland Press. He is the author of *A Possible Contemporary Poetry* (Makar Press, 1982).

P.S. I got a first for my MAThesis and a scholarship to do a PhD at the Northern Territory Uni = $13,000 tax free for 3 yrs, so I'm pretty chuffed.
Love to everyone Lys.

The honey-ant men's love song

and other Aboriginal song poems

edited by

RMW Dixon and Martin Duwell

University of Queensland Press

First published 1990 by University of Queensland Press
Box 42, St Lucia, Queensland 4067 Australia
Reprinted 1990

Typeset by University of Queensland Press
Printed in Australia by Globe Press, Melbourne

Distributed in the USA and Canada by
International Specialized Book Services, Inc.,
5602 N.E. Hassalo Street, Portland, Oregon 97213-3640

Cataloguing in Publication Data
National Library of Australia
The Honey-ant men's love song and other Aboriginal song poems.

  [1]. Aboriginal Australian poetry. [2₃. Aboriginal
  Australian poetry — Translations into English. I.
  Dixon, R.M.W. (Robert Malcolm Ward), 1939-   . II.
  Duwell, Martin, 1948-

899.15

ISBN 0 7022 2278 X

Songs performed by

Paddy Biran
Pompey Clumppoint
Frank Gurrmanamana
Spider Henry
Thomas Jangala
Mick McLean
Frank Malkorda
Johnny Mundrugmundrug
Jimmy Murray
Tom Murray
Maudie Naylon
Jacky Riala
Jimmy Russell
Leslie Russell
George Watson

Songs recorded and translated by

Margaret Clunies Ross
R.M.W. Dixon
Luise A. Hercus
Stephen A. Wild

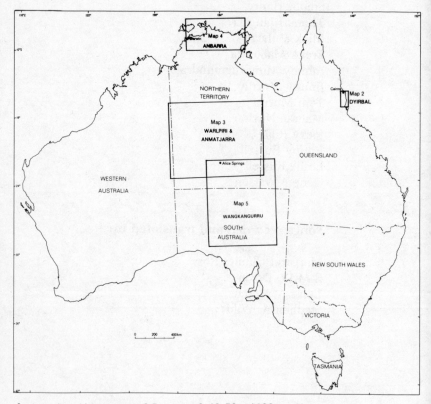

1 Australia, with key to maps 2-5 on pages 2, 48, 72 and 106

Contents

Some Dyirbal Songs – R.M.W. Dixon

A Central Australian Men's Love Song
  – Stephen A. Wild

Some Anbarra Songs – Margaret Clunies Ross

Some Wangkangurru Songs – Luise A. Hercus

Maps

Notes on the Performers and Translators

Paddy Biran (Garranba) was born around the early 1920s. He had an unparalleled knowledge of traditional legends and songs, and was also a most active and original composer. He recorded three Girramay stories and half-a-dozen songs one afternoon in 1964, and a few months later was tragically killed, when thrown off the back of a truck as it overturned on a slippery corner.

Pompey Clumppoint was a member of the Jirru tribe from Clump Point, just across from Dunk Island. He was sent by the Queensland police to live on Palm Island, away from his tribal land. Besides being a renowned songman, he was also a skilled maker of traditional artefacts. He died in the early 1970s, aged 80 or more.

Margaret Clunies Ross was born Margaret Tidemann in Adelaide in 1942 and was educated at the Universities of Adelaide and Oxford. She has been a member of the English Department at Sydney University since 1969 where she teaches Old English, Old Icelandic and the Aboriginal Performing Arts. Her research interests include Old Icelandic literature and myth and Aboriginal songs and oral literature.

R.M.W. (Bob) Dixon was born in England in 1939 and has been Professor of Linguistics at the Australian National University since 1970. He has written grammars of four Australian languages from North Queensland and studied the kinship system and the language of songs. Among his publications are *The Languages of Australia* (Cambridge University Press, 1980) and *Searching for Aboriginal Languages* (UQP, 1983).

Frank Gurrmanamana was born about 1925 and grew up in Arnhem Land in the Blyth River region. During World War II he walked into Darwin with a group of young Anbarra men and worked for a time for the Armed Forces. When the government settlement of Maningrida was established in the late 1950s, Gurrmanamana went to live there with his family. He now divides his time between Maningrida and the Blyth River. He has been a senior singer of Djambidj since the early 1970s.

Spider Henry (Ngarrguny) was born about 1920 and partly brought up by Hughie Henry, a white settler at Bellenden near Tully; he also became an expert on tribal customs and songs. He is the last remaining Gubi, or "wise man" of the Jirrbal people.

Luise A. Hercus was born in Europe in 1926 and now teaches Sanskrit at the Australian National University. She first started studying Australian languages in Victoria and in far western New South Wales in 1963 and has specialised in linguistic "salvage" work. For the last twenty years she has been studying the traditions of the northern Lake Eyre basin.

Thomas Jangala was born about 1940 near Granites, Northern Territory, on the western edge of the Tanami Desert in traditional Warlpiri country. Since the establishment of the Aboriginal settlements of Yuedumu and Lajamanu (formerly Hooker Creek) after World War II he has lived in both places at different times. He is very active in traditional ceremonial life, and is an accomplished singer and dancer.

Mick McLean (Irinjili) was born about 1888 at the Pirlakaya well in the central Simpson Desert. He had complete command of the Wangkangurru language and of Lower Southern Aranda, as well as a vast store of knowledge of the mythology and songs of the northeast of South Australia. He was a most widely respected man whose varied career included eight years in Adelaide as the main police "black tracker" (about 1920-28) and many years as head stockman on Stuart Creek Station. He died in Port Augusta in 1977.

Frank Malkorda was born about 1930 and grew up in Arnhem Land in the Blyth River region. His father was Nakarra and his mother was a member of the Burarra-speaking Anbarra people. He lives at the outstation of Gorrong-gorrong, near his patrilineal estate, not far from Maningrida, and is a Djambidj singer and a widely respected ritual leader in north-central Arnhem Land.

Johnny Mundrugmundrug was born about 1928 at Mardangajirra, which is his clan estate, and which lies a little to the east of the Blyth River. He died in Darwin in 1987 and is buried on his estate. He was a highly respected singer of Goyulan and a bark painter of some repute. He grew up in the bush but as a young man spent some time at Milingimbi Mission, where he learned to sing Goyulan from an older master. In recent decades he divided his time between Maningrida, Darwin and the Blyth River.

Jimmy Murray (Girrinyjany) was born in the 1890s and died in the late 1960s. Although living away from home for many years as a police tracker at Bowen, he was acknowledged to be the leading composer and performer of Girramay songs.

Tom Murray was born in the early 1920s and brought up by his father in a semi-nomadic life not attached to any white settlement. He has spent a good deal of his life working for cattle stations in western Queensland but has now retired to live at Mount Garnet. He remembers many of the traditional Jirrbal songs he was taught as a boy.

Maudie Naylon (Akawiljika) was born in the Simpson Desert about 1886. She was the last survivor of those who had known traditional Wangkangurru country, and she represented the last direct link with the desert. As a young woman she lived at the Killalpaninna Mission and acquired a knowledge of Ngamini, Yawarawarrka and Yarluyandi. These languages became extinct when she died in Birdsville in 1981.

Jacky Riala is a member of a clan whose estate is at Kopanga, on the west bank of the Blyth River. This clan owns the song series Goyulan and both Riala and his brother Mirribanga are well-known as Goyulan singers. Riala was born about 1940 and lives in the township of Maningrida.

Jimmy Russell (Wangamirri) was born in 1903 and died in 1988; his cousin **Leslie Russell** (Wangapulanha) was born in 1910 and died in 1975. They were the last people with a knowledge of Wangkatjaka, the form of Wangkangurru once spoken in the lower Diamantina and the Kallakoopah Rivers, on the southern margins of the Simpson Desert.

George Watson (Nyiyija) was born about 1899 at Jordan's Creek, and brought up in the tribal way by his Mamu grandfather. He has worked in the timber and cattle industries, and has been a police sergeant on Palm Island. George Watson is respected by all the Aboriginal people of the Atherton tablelands region as a prime authority on traditional languages, customs and songs.

Stephen A. Wild was born in Perth, Western Australia, in 1941. After studying Western music at the University of Western Australia, he completed his doctorate in anthropology at Indiana University, with a thesis on Warlpiri music and dance. He taught at Monash University and at the City University of New York, and is now Ethnomusicology Research Officer at the Australian Institute of Aboriginal Studies.

Introduction

> *Ngaa . . .* now then
> mist which lies across the country
> a bulldozer nosing into Guymay-nginbi
> dynamite which exploded
> the place becoming cleared
> mist which lies across the country
> a bulldozer nosing into Guymay-nginbi
> dynamite which exploded
>
> *Ahh . . .*
> my father's father's country
> I had to sing about it
> mist which lies across the country
> the place becoming cleared
> a bulldozer nosing into Guymay-nginbi
> dynamite which exploded
> *Ahh . . .* mist which lies over the country
>
> mist which lies over the country
> dynamite which exploded
> the place becoming cleared
> I had to sing about
> my father's father's country
> dynamite which exploded
> a bulldozer nosing into Guymay-nginbi
> mist which lies across the country
> dynamite which exploded

The appearance of poems such as this one, Paddy Biran's song, in *The Collins Book of Australian Poetry* marked a watershed in Australian poetry. Some of the enormous body of Aboriginal songs, both ceremonial and topical, had been translated but these had been seen as primarily anthropological documents. Rodney Hall's decision to begin his anthology with "The Moon Bone Song of the Wonguri-Mandjigai" and to include poems such as Paddy Biran's extraordinary lament has helped to widen our image of Australian poetry to the point where we finally see poetry originally composed in English as only one of the many powerful and competing traditions in Australia. This tendency was confirmed in Les A. Murray's important anthology *The New Oxford Book of Australian Verse*. As a result, readers of Australian poetry have, in the past few years, shown a desire to find satisfactory translations of at least a part of the rich body of Aboriginal oral literature. This book is an attempt to respond to that desire.

Before the white invasion there were six or seven hundred different tribes in Australia speaking between them over two hundred languages (each as distinct as French and German). Song was, as it still is, a central component of Aboriginal culture, often marking the connection between a people and their country. Compositions which are attributed to the dreamtime ancestors may well encapsulate both law and history. They will be performed in a ritual context, accompanied by dance and decoration, and will provoke deep religious feelings. These songs appear in an amazing diversity of styles, probably rather more than in the whole of Europe. All we are presenting is a small selection from each of four groups. But it should provide a hint of the overall diversity – from the strict metrical patterns of Dyirbal songs to the interwoven song cycles of the Wangkangurru or to the Anbarra song series from which a selection may be made at any recital.

Compromises are necessary in making available poems from this, the "senior culture" of Australia (as Les A. Murray so felicitously describes it), within a European framework. That which was handed down through the generations by word of mouth and which was performed by a group of people in a formal setting amid a communal sense of passion and ecstacy, must be translated for one person, who may be sitting alone in his or her living room. And for a person with different cultural norms, fears, beliefs, and expectations. Part of the original symbolism should still be apparent but its impact will inevitably be muted; nevertheless we feel that much of the essence of this rich art form survives transfer into another world.

It has been necessary to translate not only the words but also the form of each composition – into verses and lines, which are the units of poetry in the European tradition. The various translators in this volume have approached the task in different ways. For the Love Song from Central Australia, Stephen A. Wild has identified lines on semantic grounds, rather than from the form of the original. For the Dyirbal songs, R.M.W. Dixon has equated "line" with the repeatable unit of performance, and a "verse" division with where a speaker paused for breath or for a musical interlude. All the translators have done some editing (of repetitions, for example) to produce something which is both an appropriate interpretation of the original and also an accessible poem in English.

As with English poetry, Aboriginal songs have special linguistic characteristics. They may use different grammatical frames from the spoken language and there is often a special "song vocabulary" which may include some archaic forms. An important song would sometimes be transmitted across political boundaries and might be performed by people who did not fully understand the language in which it was composed (something like the performance of the Mass in Latin).

We have followed the style of other University of Queensland Press editions of non-English language Australian poetry by including the original language text along with its translation. We felt that it was appropriate to add brief notes on the various styles and on the songs themselves, in order to sketch in a cultural context. The original version of Paddy Biran's song, which is an intense lament in the Jangala style, is delivered at a fast and angry tempo, something that might not be guessed when reading the song in translation. We suggest that the reader first look at the translations as poems in their own right, then read the local introductions and notes and finally reread the poems with the added depth these supply.

R.M.W. Dixon
Martin Duwell

A Note on Pronunciation

The original songs have been written in phonemic orthographies. Most letters have much the same value as in English (g being hard, as in gate). The vowel *i* is generally pronounced "ee" as in *beet*, *u* as "oo" in *boot*, and *a* like the vowel in *bat*.

Sounds in these languages which differ from English are (i) retroflexes, with the tongue turned back in the mouth (as in Indian languages and in Indian pronunciation of English) are shown by *rd, rt, rn, rl*; (ii) dentals, with the tongue touching the top teeth, are shown by *dh, th, nh, lh;* (iii) *ng* represents the sound [ŋ], which occurs only at the end of a word in English, as in *sing* and *bang*; the sequence [ŋg], as in *finger*, is always written *-ngg-;* (iv) most Australian languages have two *r*-sounds − *rr* is used to represent a trill (as in Scottish pronunciations of English) while *r* is used for a continuant sound, not too different from the *r*-sound in Australian English; Wangkangurru has three different *r*-sounds, with *rr* being used for a trill, *r* for a flap and *R* for a continuant.

In the spoken language styles of Dyirbal, Walbiri and Wangkangurru the first syllable of a word bears major stress; for the Anbarra, major stress generally goes on the first syllable of the root (which may be preceded by prefixes). Some song styles carry a quite different pattern of accentuation from the spoken language (see the introductory notes on Dyirbal styles). For Wangkangurru, Luise Hercus has marked all stressed syllables with an acute accent.

Some Dyirbal Songs

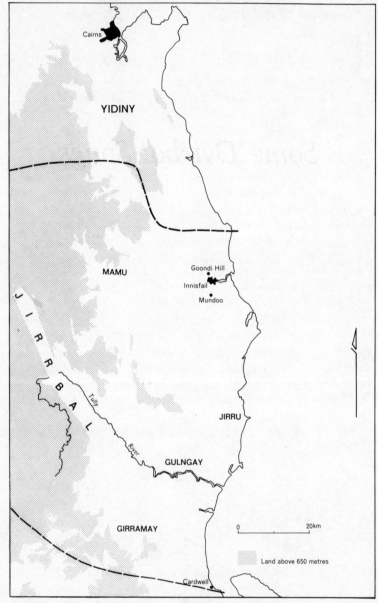

2   The Dyirbal language (with dialects Mamu, Jirrbal, Jirru, Gulngay and Girramay) and the Yidiny language

Some Dyirbal Songs

The Dyirbal language was spoken by a group of six contiguous tribes in the Cairns rainforest region of North Queensland. There are two categories of song, which speakers of Dyirbal nowadays refer to as "corroboree songs" and "love songs".

Corroboree songs deal with everyday topics. Any noteworthy scene or event may be the inspiration for an evocative song (with no deeper message implied). When several tribes met together, a male singer would stand holding two boomerangs each by its middle and clap the ends together as accompaniment. Several women would crouch nearby, each banging a skin drum that was stretched across her thighs. A number of male dancers, appropriately decorated, would mime the event described in the song.

Love songs were also known as Gugulu, from the name of the main hardwood accompaniment stick, which gives out a resonant note when held vertically and hit with a piece of lawyer cane. A Gugulu song is likely to convey a personal message – typically of love, jealousy or revenge, dealing with a topic about which the singer feels strongly. Gugulu songs could be performed at any time, by men or women, either privately to one person or else semi-publicly. Some of the listeners might improvise a dance in shake-a-leg style – a vigorous solo dance with the dancer's legs spread wide apart – although there need be no dance accompaniment.

R.M.W. Dixon

Gama Style

The most popular of the corroboree styles is called Gama. Like all Dyirbal song styles, this has a strict metre. Each line in a Gama song has either nine or eleven syllables.

A Gama line divides into three distinct parts:

• the first portion has five syllables, with stress on the first and fourth. It may be one five-syllable word or a two-syllable and a three-syllable word;

• the second portion (only included if the line has eleven syllables) is a two-syllable word with stress on the first syllable;

• the final portion is one four-syllable word, with stress going onto first and last syllables.

There may be just two lines, alternated many times (with a pause for breath after every third line) or there can be slightly more complex patterns, as in the examples which follow.

The Red Gown

Gawun gurigu ngana gunggamburrgu
Gawun gurigu ngana yamalyamal
Gawun gurigu ngana gunggamburrgu

Gawun gurigu ngana waga-nyurriny
Gawun gurigu ngana yamalyamal
Gawun gurigu ngana gunggamburrgu

Gawun gurigu ngana waga-nyurriny
Gawun gurigu ngana yamalyamal
Gawun gurigu ngana gunggamburrgu
Gawun gurigu ngana waga-nyurriny

In the very early days of contact, Aborigines saw a white girl wearing a red dress with white spots. They had never seen anything quite like this and made up a song about it, with dancers imitating the movements of the girl.

The Red Gown

The red gown we see is like a butterfly
A red gown that catches the eye
The red gown we see is like a butterfly

Red gown dancing in joy
A red gown that catches the eye
The red gown we see is like a butterfly

Red gown dancing in joy
A red gown that catches the eye
The red gown we see is like a butterfly
Red gown dancing in joy

Jimmy Murray, 1967
(Girramay dialect)

Thunder

Mungga walmanyu murrul ngumarrangu
Murrul walmanyu mungga ngumarrangu
Mada nyiburu gubu guraragu

Mina milmindu minba mayjalagu
Mungga walmanyu murrul ngumarrangu
Mada nyiburu gubu guraragu

Mungga walmanyu murrul ngumarrangu
Mada nyiburu gubu guraragu
Mina milmindu minba mayjalagu
Mungga walmanyu murrul ngumarrangu

It is believed that armpit sweat (gurara) has special properties. Rubbed onto a sick person it can help effect a cure. And a leaf soaked in armpit sweat, hurled in the face of a storm, may arrest the thunder and lightning.

Thunder

A mighty noise rises up, roars as it rushes by
Rushes and rises, a mighty noise that roars
Hurl out a leaf that is soaked in sweat

Bolts of lightning strike, and flare
A mighty noise rises up, roars as it rushes by
Hurl out a leaf that is soaked in sweat

A mighty noise rises up, roars as it rushes by
Hurl out a leaf that is soaked in sweat
Bolts of lightning strike, and flare
A mighty noise rises up, roars as it rushes by

Jimmy Murray, 1967
(Girramay dialect)

Baby Cockatoos

Mulungga ngari balnggaybalnggay
Guwal girrmanyu jagalinyu

Mulungga ngari balnggaybalnggay
Guwal girrmanyu jagalinyu
Yiranbarragu budingugu

Mulungga ngari balnggaybalnggay
Guwal girrmanyu jagalinyu
Yiranbarragu budingugu

White cockatoo chicks sit in their nest, in a hollow log,
crying out in hunger.

Baby Cockatoos

Waiting hopefully in the end of a hollow log
They swallow noisily, their voices beg

Waiting hopefully in the end of a hollow log
They swallow noisily, their voices beg
For the food their mother brings

Waiting hopefully in the end of a hollow log
They swallow noisily, their voices beg
For the food their mother brings

Pompey Clumppoint, 1964
(Jirru dialect)

Jangala Style

Jangala is one of the Gugulu or "love song" styles. These songs describe some intense feeling, or a particularly significant event.

Each line in a Jangala song consists of six syllables. It can be made up of a two-syllable and a four-syllable word or two three-syllable words or one six-syllable word. (Dyirbal has only a handful of monosyllabic words, and these are not used in songs.) Each word is stressed on its first syllable, as in normal spoken Dyirbal.

Jangala songs have a number of lines which may be repeated in variable order, the only proviso being that two lines which belong together grammatically (making up one sentence) should occur contiguously, in either order.

Shifting Camp

Yilmburrinyu yirri
Galbarrayarranyu
Gunggarimu janggirr
Jarrugan bunangan
Gunggarrimu janggirr
Jarrugan bunangan
Yimanbangu gabi
Gulnggangu barrbandal
Yidiny-yidiny guwal
Jayanu yadanyu
Walmbinamu julnggay

Walmbinamu julnggay
Ngawaru Yidinyba
Guwal balan Mamu

In traditional days, a young girl was sometimes seized by a man from another tribe and carried off; the song refers to a Mamu girl taken to live with the Yidiny people. She would learn the language of her husband as well as retaining something of her parents' language, and her children would be taught something of both languages. This is likened to the scrub-hen, a bird that constructs a high mound to incubate its eggs. The scrub-hen may not build its nest twice in the same location, moving from one place one season to another the next. After building all day, it will at dusk shake a fig tree to dislodge the fruit. The two parts of the song are linked by the verb gulngga-, *in the eighth line, which refers to a woman giving birth to a child, and here also to a tree bearing fruit.*

Shifting Camp

Dragging leaves for its nest
Calling out, after nest building
As daylight fades from the north
The scrub-hen, travelling far
As daylight fades from the north
The scrub-hen, travelling far
Shakes the branches of the fig-tree
Women, like the tree, bear fruit
Talk Yidiny all the time
Strangers, who scarcely recall their parents' tongue
Crossing borders, travelling on

Crossing borders, travelling on
They speak Yidiny with one voice
And Mamu with another

Tom Murray, 1984
(Jirrbal dialect)

15

Goondi Hill

Gubigubi bunu
Gandangu gulbarru
Mabin birri gabi
Wulmburrunngunuga
Gubigubi bunu

Bunu gubigubi
Mabin birri gabi
Wulmburrunngunuga
Danggal banday mirra
Buran gulu ngaygu
Mirra banagaymban
Birrmaymban Gundigu

Bunu gubigubi
Gandangu gulbarru
Buran gulu ngaygu
Mabin birri gabi
Wulmburrunngunugu
Danggal banday mirra

A Girramay man has visited Goondi Hill, just north of Innisfail (in Mamu territory) and fallen in love with it. As he journeys home, dawn breaks through the jungle. Through the flapping wings of a giant bird (said to have lived at Innisfail in days gone by) he looks back, with warmth, at Goondi Hill.

Goondi Hill

As daylight was coming up
As the dawn began to glow
As if through a dark cloud
Through the jungle foliage
As daylight was coming up

As daylight was coming up
As if through a dark cloud
Through the jungle foliage
A wing flapping in front
I didn't look towards my own land
But turned around
And looked back at Goondi Hill

As daylight was coming up
As the dawn began to glow
I didn't look towards my own land
As if through a dark cloud
Through the jungle foliage
A wing flapping in front

George Watson, 1964
(Mamu dialect)

Staggering Man

Barrmi nganya bula
Gundinggu ngulburu
Yugu gulgurrunda
Gulgugulgugabi
Waga nganya muya
Bajingu daymbingu
Yugu gulgurrunda
Gulgugulgugabi

Gulgugulgugabi
Barrmi nganya bula
Gundinggu ngulburu
Nyijirrnyijirubi
Waga nganya muya
Bajingu daymbingu
Yugu gulgurrunda

Yugu gulgurrunda
Gulgugulgugabi
Barrmi nganya bula
Gundinggu ngulburu
Nyijirrnyijirubi
Waga nganya muya

Waga nganya muya
Bajingu daymbingu
Yugu gulgurrunda
Gulgugulgugabi

Barrmi nganya bula
Gulgugulgugabi

The singer has gone on a walk in the bush with his wife and her classificatory sister (who is also a potential wife for him). He is drunk, falling down in the undergrowth. As his wife's sister smiles seductively at him, all he is able to do is stagger and tumble over logs that lie across the path.

Staggering Man

The two of them look back at me
One is glancing sideways, through half-closed eyes
I fall among the logs
All in a heap
My legs are shakey
As I stagger, move groggily
I fall among the logs
All in a heap

All in a heap
The two of them look back at me
One is glancing sideways, through half-closed eyes
That one smiles in invitation
My legs are shakey
As I stagger, move groggily
I fall among the logs

I fall among the logs
All in a heap
The two of them look back at me
One is glancing sideways, through half-closed eyes
That one smiles in invitation
But my legs are shakey

My legs are shakey
As I stagger, move groggily
I fall among the logs
All in a heap

The two of them look back at me
All in a heap

Paddy Biran, 1964
(Girramay dialect)

Cutting a Track to Cardwell

Yalgay juburrbara
Nudingu bilbara
Yabuyabungunu
Jayaringunubi
Garuwulgu yunggul
Bagala mijingu
Bungalbungalgubi

Yunggul Garuwulgu
Bagala mijingu
Bungalbungalgubi

Gurrgagurrga yugu
Muyulu julnggari
Yugu gurrgagurrga
Muyulu julnggari
Balgarugumbangu
Nudingu gaymbingu
Gunarrundu warja
Mayirra nyarrunda
Warja gunarrunda
Mayirra nyarrunda
Bunggubunggugubi
Wunggu bandangurru
Jarrarringurrubi

The early white settlers established cattle stations over the range, and had to cut a track down to the port of Cardwell. This song describes the white men, assisted by Aborigines, cutting the track, and then waiting at Cardwell for a boat, looking out and glimpsing Palm Island (where there was a "mission"). The white men worked quickly, talking all the time to each other in their own, strange tongue.

Cutting a Track to Cardwell

The track is cleared
Trees have been cut down, for the highway
As a mother carries her child
So the horse bears its rider
To Cardwell, along a single track
We can see across the ocean to the mission
Having just come down the range

Along a single track to Cardwell
We can see across the ocean to the mission
Having just come down the range

A wide swath of trees
Cut to ground level
Trees in a wide swath
Cut to ground level
With steel axes
Cut so quickly
By a mob of men, chattering in English
Their voices echoing
English, spoken by a mob of men
Their voices echoing
As they work close together
Lips slapping as they talk
All talking at the same time

Tom Murray, 1983
(Jirrbal dialect)

She Will Not Go With Me

Maya ngaygunalay
Nyandumi bambanyu
Burraranyu nyandu
Nyandumi bambanyu

Nyandumi bambanyu
Burraranyu nyandu
Ngaygunalay maya
Burraranyu nyandu
Yibul jabirrinyu
Marruru gulnginyu

Marruru gulnginyu
Maya ngaygunalay
Birabin mulngganyu

Birabin mulngganyu
Burraranyu nyandu
Maya ngaygunalay

Marriages were arranged many years in advance; a young girl (from the appropriate kinship class) would be "promised" to an older man. The song describes a man coming to claim his bride — but she, not knowing him at all, recoils in fright, refuses the marriage, and wishes to go instead with the boy she loves (who is not, in any case, in the right kinship class for her to marry).

She Will Not Go with Me

No, she will not go with me
She doesn't know me, isn't used to me
She turns away, not knowing me
She doesn't know me, isn't used to me

She doesn't know me, isn't used to me
She turns away, not knowing me
She will not go with me, no
She turns away, not knowing me
Refuses to be my wife
Wants someone she cannot have, and rejects me

Wants someone she cannot have, and rejects me
No, she will not go with me
She's scared, she's petrified with fright

She's scared, she's petrified with fright
She turns away, not knowing me
No, she will not go with me

Jimmy Murray, 1967
(Girramay dialect)

King Tide Receding

Balangali janyja
Jajingu ganagu
Balangali janyja
Dumbulanmigubi
Balangali janyja

Balangali janyja
Jajingu ganagu
Dumbulanmigubi
Balangali banggul
Ngangu jarbarrubi
Buynggangu ganagu

A king tide has come high up on the beach and now, as it recedes, it looks as if there is a huge water spout at Dumbulanmi (a place where, in legend, the skin of a dead person was once found) sucking the tide back into the ocean.

King Tide Receding

The tide is down there now
Moving back to the middle of the ocean
The tide is down there now
There is a water spout at Dumbulanmi
The tide is down there now

The tide is down there now
Moving back to the middle of the ocean
And the water spout at Dumbulanmi
Down there, it is like
The mouth of a wide dilly-bag
As it sucks the tide back into the middle of the ocean

Spider Henry, 1982
(Jirrbal dialect)

Dry Throat

Ngayi ngayba jida
Jangala jinbala
Ngayi jirajira
Gilngaragu maya
Gudangu garrindu

Gudangu garrindu
Marrimarrigubi
Banggu nyurranginyju

Banggu nyurranginyju
Gudan gilngaragu
Marrimarrigubi
Malanggumbangurru

Malanggumbangurru
Marrany mangurrubi
Banggu nyurranginyju
Gilngaragu gudan

Gudan gilngaragu
Marrimarrigubi
Ngayi jirajira
Jinbalambangubi

The singer has a bad cold, which he has caught from the people to whom he addresses this Jangala song. His throat is dry and he can scarcely sing, even though he works clay under water with his hands and applies it to his throat as a poultice.

Dry Throat

My throat is dry
Too sore to sing Jangala
A thick, dry throat
A bad cold grips me
The cold blocks my throat

The cold blocks my throat
Such a heavy cold
Caught from you people

Caught from you people
The cold impedes me
Such a heavy cold
With my hands, under water

With my hands, under water
I work clay, for a poultice
Caught from you people
The cold impedes me

The cold impedes me
Such a heavy cold
A thick, dry throat
And I cannot sing properly

Jimmy Murray, 1967
(Girramay dialect)

The Brave Husband

Manggu bulgamugu
Jalbarra mugabiny
Guyabay mabilma
Wugiru balngayju

Wugiru balngayju
Jungalugu banggul
Nguju jubingarra

Nguju jubingarra
Guyabay mabilma
Wugiru balngayju

Wugiru balngayju
Dayigu girmanda
Manggu bulgamugu
Jalbarra mugabiny

Manggu bulgamugu
Jalbara mugabiny
Guyabay mabilma
Gamu juganuga
Galgalbara mabi

A couple are crossing the river together. But the wife cannot swim and the waters are rough and dangerous. At the halfway mark her husband lifts her high and carries her to the far bank, ostentatiously showing off his bravery.

The Brave Husband

Grasping her arms with his strong hands
Halfway across the rough stream
He takes her to the other side
Showing off his courage

Showing off his courage
Carrying her on his shoulder
As the dirty water swirls by

As the dirty water swirls by
He takes her to the other side
Showing off his courage

Showing off his courage
Holding her high, by the wrists
Grasping her arms with his strong hands
Halfway across the rough stream

Grasping her arms with his strong hands
Halfway across the rough stream
He takes her to the other side
In the fast-flowing water
Crossing through the clayey stream

Jimmy Murray, 1967
(Girramay dialect)

A Camp Tainted by Death

Yanggu nyurranginyju
Buga bungalugu
Gabugabugubi
Nguji bungalumany

Nguji bungalumany
Warrburraymbangubi
Yabandayju nganya

Yabandayju nganya
Buga bungalugu
Gabugabugubi

Gabugabugubi
Yimburr nyurranginyju
Yabandayju nganya
Buga bungalugu

*When someone dies all of their possessions and the camp where they were living
are said to be* bungalu, *tainted by death, and thus tabooed. The singer here
tells his audience that their camp is* bungalu, *because of a recent death there,
and that they should move on.*

A Camp Tainted by Death

This place belonging to all of you
Has the rotten smell of one who has died
A filthy smell
A place tainted by death

A place tainted by death
Making me tired and lifeless
It is the camp which affects me

It is the camp which affects me
The rotten smell of one who has died
A filthy smell

A filthy smell
A stink like a turtle, in your place
It is the camp which affects me
The rotten smell of one who has died

Jimmy Murray, 1967
(Girramay dialect)

Burran Style

Burran is another Gugulu or "love song" style, describing something that has stirred strong emotions.

A Burran song generally has four lines — one of six syllables, then three syllables, then another of six, and a final line of three syllables. As in the Jangala style, and in spoken Dyirbal, the first syllable of each word is stressed.

The lines of a Burran song may be sung — generally, in strict sequence — twenty or more times in succession, with the voice rising and falling in loudness. There is often a final coda — *eee, aaa, ooo*.

The Dwarf

Wawujilu ngaja
Mirrubin
Yinban dalaragu
Bayangu
Wawujilu ngaja
Mirrubin
Yinban dalaragu
Bayangu
Wawujilu ngaja
    eee, aaa, ooo

Dyirbal has a word mirru *(dwarf), referring to a child that never grows to adult
stature. It was believed that such a condition could be due to a sorcerer
"singing" at the victim. Dwarfs were often laughed at — but in this song the
dwarf has the last laugh, describing the sorcerer who sang about him as being
like a locust.*

The Dwarf

No wonder that I am
A child that never grew
That man is a locust
Singing me
No wonder that I am
A child that never grew
That man is a locust
Singing me
No wonder that I am
eee, aaa, ooo

George Watson, 1982
(Mamu dialect)

Sugar Train

Mandungunu bunga
Jugagu
Gangalbira waynyji
Riluway
Mandungunu bunga
Jugagu
Gangalbira waynyji
Riluway
Mandungunu bunga
Jugagu
Gangalbira waynyji
      aaa, eee, ooo

Aborigines observed a tram bound for the sugar mill, gliding down a hill at Mundoo (near Innisfail) and then labouring to ascend the hill beyond.

Sugar Train

Going downhill from Mundoo
For sugar
Making a noise as it climbs the hill
The railway
Going downhill from Mundoo
For sugar
Making a noise as it climbs the hill
The railway
Going downhill from Mundoo
For sugar
Making a noise as it climbs the hill
aaa, eee, ooo

George Watson, 1984
(Mamu dialect)

A Craving

Walgi yagirraga
Ginmanyu
Bangun bajambajam
Jilbarri
Walgi yagirraga
Burungga
Bangun bajambajam
Jilbarri
Walgi yagirraga
Burungga
Bangun bajambajam
     eee, aaa, ooo

A pregnant woman craves possum meat. Her husband searches in the right sort of tree for yabi, *the possum — which is here called by the special song word* jilbarri.

A Craving

Look around in the blue gum tree
She's asking for food
For a possum of her fancy
Call it *jilbarri*
Look around in the blue gum tree
In a hollow of the tree
For a possum of her fancy
Call it *jilbarri*
Look around in the blue gum tree
In a hollow of the tree
For a possum of her fancy
          eee, aaa, ooo

          George Watson, 1982
           (Mamu dialect)

Song to Make Her Grow

Burrandu
Yanggu yanggu ngaja
Burrandu
Bilbaymali burrmbil
Bayali
Yanggu yanggu ngaja
Burrandu
Bilbaymali burrmbil
Bayali
Yanggu yanggu ngaja
Burrandu
Bilbaymali burrmbil
Bayali
Yanggu yanggu ngaja
Burrandu

A man may claim his "promised" wife when she is about ten and take her to live in his camp. But he may not sleep with her until she reaches puberty. A man sang this song to his child bride to make her grow quickly.

Song to Make Her Grow

In the Burran style
I am singing in this style
In the Burran style
To make the young girl grow
This is how I must sing
I am singing in this style
In the Burran style
To make the young girl grow
This is how I must sing
I am singing in this style
In the Burran style
To make the young girl grow
This is how I must sing
I am singing in this style
In the Burran style

Tom Murray, 1988
(Jirrbal dialect)

Into the Waves

Bunggugu
Jinbi yagundayi
Nayili
Jinbi yagundayi
Bunggugu
Jaburr banda burul
Bunggugu
Jinbi yagundayi
Nayili
Jaburr banda burul
Bunggugu
Jinbi yagundayi
Nayili
Jinbi yagundayi
Nayili
Jaburr banda burrul

A love-struck man lies on the beach, watching nubile young girls play in the foam, jumping into waves and making them "burst". By social convention, he could not go in too.

Into the Waves

Into the waves
Jumping up into the water
The teenage girls
Jumping up into the water
Into the waves
Foam and spray bursting
Into the waves
Jumping up into the water
The teenage girls
Foam and spray bursting
Into the waves
Jumping up into the water
The teenage girls
Jumping up into the water
The teenage girls
Foam and spray bursting

George Watson, 1963
(Jirru dialect)

His True Feelings

Jimbanyurru burul
Janayman
Wayba gunggarrigu
Ngarunggu
Jimbanyurru burul
Janayman
Wayba gunggarrigu
Ngarunggu
Jimbanyurru burul
Janayman
Wayba gunggarrigu
Ngarunggu
Jimbanyurru burul

An Aboriginal man has been given charge of the white boss's horse. He grabs the bridle and stands holding it, then does a shake-a-leg dance venting his feelings towards the white man (who is in the north), wanting to kill him.

His True Feelings

Catching hold of the bridle
Standing with it
Hating him in the north
Dancing shake-a-leg
Catching hold of the bridle
Standing with it
Hating him in the north
Dancing shake-a-leg
Catching hold of the bridle
Standing with it
Hating him in the north
Dancing shake-a-leg
Catching hold of the bridle

George Watson, 1964
(Gulngay dialect)

A Central Australian
Men's Love Song

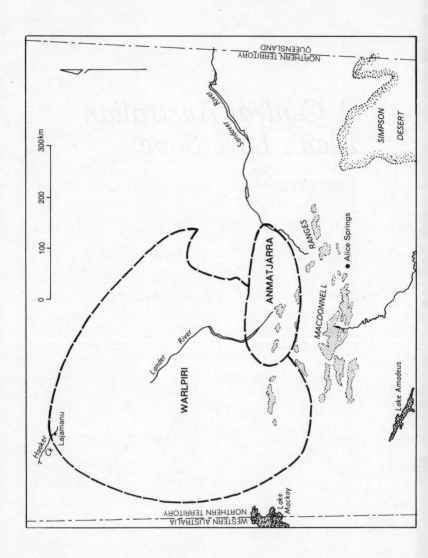

Central Australian Men's Love Song
(Yilpinji)

This song with its sixty-five verses was recorded by Thomas
Jangala at Lajamanu (formerly Hooker Creek), Northern
Territory in 1971. Although the singer is a member of the
Warlpiri language community, the song was said by him to be
Anmatjarra *(Yanmajirri* in Warlpiri), a neighbouring language
to Warlpiri.

Yilpinji, which may be translated as love songs, are a genre
owned by both men and women separately. Men's *yilpinji* may
be performed either as a large-scale ceremony exclusively and
secretly by men with full body decoration of ritual fluff, and
dancing, or privately and much less elaborately, with no fluff
decoration. Men's *yilpinji* may also be sung solo, and it is the
only men's song genre that is performed in this way. Com-
monly, however, *yilpinji* are sung by two or three singers
together. They are sung to activate Dreaming power to attract
women to men, or to put it another way, to make men attractive to women. When sung by two or three men, one is con-
cerned with making himself attractive to a particular woman
− calling out her name during the singing − while the other
two men may act as go-betweens.

These songs are rarely explicitly sexual or erotic, rather
they are clothed in the imagery of the Dreaming ancestors
which may be part human and part non-human (usually
natural species). The Dreaming ancestor Honey-Ant is the
main character in this song. The other characters are the
woman he desires and a non-human messenger or go-between
− a red bird. According to the singer, the red bird is a particular species. A man may raise it from a chick and release it
after he has performed *yilpinji*. The bird is believed to go to
the woman with the message of his desire for her. Since I was
unable to identify the species I used the term "Red Bird
Messenger" to convey both its function and its mythopoetic
role in the song. The song words constantly shift between

objective and subjective points of view, as if the singer is sometimes taking the part of each character and at other times taking the part of an outside observer. This shifting perspective reflects the fact that the singer is both singing *about* ancestral events and participating *in* the ancestral events as an actor in the process of attracting a woman. A fusion of objective and subjective experience is a salient feature of the concept of the Dreaming: human beings are both products of the Dreaming and participants in it, and the Dreaming existed in a far-distant past as well as continuing to exist in an ever present reality.

Honey-Ant Yilpinji is more narrative in style than many Warlpiri songs. A general narrative sequence can be seen as consisting of Honey-Ant setting out on a journey (verses 1-4); Honey-Ant performing the ceremony, sending Red Bird Messenger, and the effects on the woman (verses 5-43); the aftermath, the domestic scene, and the woman settling in Honey-Ant's country (verses 44-65). Some verses can be seen as belonging in pairs or groups of three or four; for example, verses 17 and 18 concern Red Bird Messenger flying away and returning, verses 22-25 have the theme of the woman digging for honey-ants, verses 28-30 are about the captured woman and forbidden love.

Stephen A. Wild

Yurrampi Yilpinji

1. Wurnata pardakijana,
   Wurnata pardakijana,
   Wurnata winpirriyana.

2. Wirangku-wirang,
   Kinirrilanu,
   Mardijalardikirri.

3. Wurnatijingka,
   Lardajilmarra larda,
   Larrinipini.

4. Wirrpijanangka,
   Warlpajanangka.

5. Ngawilyipilyi larrana,
   Mayapirrkanata,
   Ngarraljaparra larrana.

6. Mijipi jarrana,
   Makurrungu danarra.

7. Manitirrpi-tirrpi,
   Pirrinyurrpi lininyurrpi.
   Mirrarirra pirrinyurrpi.

8. Mintilyapi-lyapi
   Lungkarrku parrku.

The singing of verse 8 affects the shirt of the singer if the shirt is coloured or patterned. (Verse 14 — below — refers to a white butterfly and affects a white shirt.) The shirt is imbued with power which in turn affects the woman to whom the power is directed. The woman follows a blue (or white) butterfly which leads her to the affected shirt. When she sees it she will be irresistibly attracted to the owner of the shirt.

Honey-Ant Men's Love Song

1. He departed with thoughts of home,
   He departed with thoughts of home,
   He departed towards another place.

2. He rose to go,
   Joyfully he went,
   Sank down when he was tired.

3. Departed, he went,
   Made ready to go,
   Camped at the next place.

4. He called out to his host,
   Wind whistled at dawn.

5. Women passed by on business,
   All stayed close together,
   Mindful of their business.

6. He admired their painting stick,
   How strong and true they painted.

7. Red Bird Messenger
   Aroused a woman struck by magic.
   They travelled on, the woman aroused.

8. She followed a blue butterfly
   Looking out from a flower.

9. Mayanpa yurrkulanupa.
   Yanupa mankinja,
   Larritingi.

10. Mawilpawilpa lananapana
    Makarta-karta, lananapana.

In verse 10 Honey-Ant saw a devil approaching the women's ceremony. It is believed that devils are attracted to ceremonies because the participants are in a state of spiritual vulnerability.

11. Lima pirrintalpirri,
    Lima, marlikitarli.

The sacred objects referred to in verse 11 are string crosses (sticks bound together at right-angles to each other in the form of a cross, with hair-string threaded diagonally between adjacent arms of the cross spiralling in a single direction — clockwise or counterclockwise — from the centre of the cross outward) which the ceremonial actor wears on each side of the head, making the crosses look like dog ears. Small string crosses worn in such a manner are used in men's yilpinji *ceremony.*

12. Malkara, ngapanja,
    Kayirrpilanu.

In verse 12 a woman notices that the man who has performed yilpinji *for her, looks and walks differently, and she guesses why. The reference to rib-bone seems merely to be a detail of the man's appearance, although rib-bones are often high-lighted in Warlpiri ceremonial designs.*

13. Makiwi nyampa,
    Makulpa dirrpa,
    Rralyulpa-rralyu.

14. Mawatilarti,
    Lanupa yanu,
    Pirlkirrimpirlki
    Lanupa yanu.

9. Abdomen swollen, Honey-Ant emerged from a hole,
   Went well satisfied,
   With eggs laid.

10. Devil with evil intent
    Came fast, directly.

11. Sacred objects came close,
    Sacred objects, like dog ears.

12. He looked different, rib-bones,
    Walked a special way.

13. He followed her tracks,
    Followed her tracks where they led,
    Watching intently.

14. She followed a white butterfly,
    Which travelled fast,
    The white butterfly
    Travelled fast.

15. Manitirrpi-tirrpila
    Dintinila ralpilparlpi,
    Lamurru-lamurru, dintinila.

16. Manitirrpi-tirrpi
    Ngalura-ngalura kujuna
    Minanji, ngalura-ngalura.

Verse 16 refers to the natural design on honey-ants, and to the design applied to a yilpinji *performer. The body of the performer is first rubbed with fat, and natural ochres are applied to the greased skin, giving it a glistening appearance.*

17. Malijalija lajijipirni,
    Mangkulurrura, lajijipirni.

18. Wangkangurrula lajijipirni,
    Malijalija lajijipirni.

After returning from his long journey (verse 18), Red Bird Messenger returns to the man who sent it thus confirming that the message was delivered. The man then knows that the woman is coming close behind.

19. Karrana, lirdurdumana,
    Najirti, purrkaru karrana.

20. Dapinga-dapingata
    Dapirrintirri.

21. Dapinangka-pinangka
    Dapirrintirri.

Napangardi (Dapingata) *and Napanangka* (Dapinangka) *(in verses 20 and 21) are the female names of two social categories in Warlpiri society which may also be used to address or refer to individuals in those categories. Honey-Ant would be related to members of each category in a different way, which would determine whether they are permitted wives or lovers, depending on his own category.*

15. Red Bird Messenger
    Aroused her, as Honey-Ant approached
    Walking slowly, the woman aroused.

16. Red Bird Messenger
    Saw the glistening design
    On Honey-Ant, glistening.

17. Then flew off on a long journey,
    Sorrowfully, a long journey.

18. He spoke after his long journey,
    He flew off on a long journey.

19. Anxious, she went anyway,
    Nothing will happen, slowly and anxiously she went.

20. Ngapangardi-Ngapangardi
    Danced all the way.

21. Napanangka-Napanangka
    Danced all the way.

22. Manima laru palpinyi,
    Japal manima laru palpinyi,
    Japal mardana laru palpinyi.

23. Mankalijanka lanupayanu,
    Mawunpurrunyu, lanupayanu.

24. Mintirrinjila lanupayanu,
    Mawunpurrunyu lanupayanu.

25. Mintirrirrinti lanupayanu,
    Mawunpurrunyu lanupayanu.

26. Makarntarrngawu,
    Mirltardimarra,
    Lanupayanu.

27. Yungkupu, yunarrinarra
    Yunarripunju.

28. Nyanuwa, januwaji,
    Nyanuwajilina,
    Jirdilkirdilkila.

29. Nyanuwa, januwaji,
    Yamurajilina,
    Jirdilkirdilkila.

30. Narrumpa jilina,
    Jijilkiwilki,
    Waljilajilina.

Verses 29 and 30 convey the fact that love ceremonies may result in illicit or immoral unions, either between a man and a woman, who is in the relationship of mother-in-law to him, or between a man and a woman who are genealogically close cross-cousins (father's sister's daughter/son or mother's brother's daughter/son). In the latter case, genealogically distant cross-cousins, that is those who call each other "cross-cousin" but cannot trace an actual genealogical relationship, may legitimately marry, but sexual relations between close cross-cousins are forbidden.

22. A large hole she dug for Honey-Ant,
    Deeply she dug for Honey-Ant,
    From the deep she retrieved from the hole.

23. Dug a hole as she journeyed,
    Squatting to dig, she journeyed.

24. Deeply she dug as she journeyed,
    Squatting to dig as she journeyed.

25. Extracted the stick as she journeyed,
    Squatting to dig, she journeyed.

26. Slowly she walked,
    Hobbling, limping,
    She journeyed.

27. Resting in shade, she sat
    And slept.

28. Lover, lover,
    Lover,
    Snared, entrapped.

29. Lover, lover,
    Mother-in-law,
    Snared, entrapped.

30. Close-cousin loved,
    Resisted,
    Forbidden love.

31. Manitirrpi-tirrpi lingampi-lingampilpinyi
    Marawingara, lingampilpinyi.

32. Mantirrpiti lanpanya-panya,
    Marawingara, lanpanya-panya.

33. Makurn pakurn,
    Palata lampanya-panya,
    Manangkiji palala, lampanya-payna.

In a men's love ceremony, a string cross is pointed horizontally in the direction of the desired woman, directing the power of the ceremony at her. In verse 33, it is Red Bird Messenger who points the string cross at her as he dances.

34. Manu yurulpa,
    Manangkiyi palala,
    Lampanya-panya.

35. Mirrijinji ridilanu,
    Mawa nupa ridilanu.

36. Lipamarra matilatila,
    Matutala.

37. Wuna jirrpilpa
    Malparranjipa,
    Ngalarangala.

31. Red Bird Messenger journeyed,
    Flew a long distance, journeyed.

32. Red Bird Messenger returned underground,
    Flew a long distance, returned underground.

33. Carrying the sacred object horizontally,
    Red Bird Messenger danced,
    Red Bird Messenger held it, danced.

34. Making the way clear,
    Red Bird Messenger held it,
    Dancing.

35. Admired her shapely legs,
    Admired her loins and eyes.

36. Eyes looked at the visitor,
    Lovesick.

37. The woman left
    Her country,
    Heavily.

38. Mirrjipirrji mungkarla,
    Tanyilingi latupatu.

Hair-string is spun onto a stick with a shorter cross-member lashed to it (verse 38). The stick is twirled between the thigh and the open palm of a hand, the other hand feeding a twisted strand of hair around the cross. The spun hair-string and cross-member are pulled off the end of the stick as a ball of string entwined on the cross-member. Hair-string is spun during men's love ceremonies, and after the spinner takes the ball of string off the stick he strikes the spinning stick on the ground while calling out the name of the desired woman. Since the hair being spun is usually the spinner's own hair, the spinning stick is imbued with his own Dreaming power which, together with the power of the song, is directed at the woman.

39. Minyirawirra malkara
    Ngajina lajapirrpini.

40. Manitirrpi-tirrpi mawalyangka,
    Lirra-lirra.

41. Ngitinja, lungkarrkuparrku,
    Nganyili, ngitinja.

42. Milpala jatarr-jatarri,
    Pilpali milpala.

43. Luyunguparti, junjukurntu-kurntu
    Marrapirarrapara.

Male initiation in central Australia is marked by two physical operations, circumcision and subincision. Verses 43 and 50 refer to subincision, the second operation, indicating that Honey-Ant is fully initiated.

44. Yapupanyiki martikijikiji
    Kajuntuluwarra ya.

45. Nyilpirta, karlpatali,
    Nyinari-nyinari la.

38. Honey-Ant spun hair-string,
    Honey-Ant struck the ground with the spinning-stick.

39. My beautiful body paint
    Will bring her to me.

40. Red Bird Messenger flew away,
    Talked to her.

41. She searched, only half-sleeping,
    She watched, she searched.

42. Heavy eyes,
    Sleepless eyes.

43. Dancing, her spirit visited
    The initiated man.

44. Plain-country person
    In mid-morning.

45. Friends, tired,
    They sat.

46. Manamalajala lyirrilarilyarra,
    Manamalajala mangkala lananyapanya.

In verse 46 Honey-Ant debates within himself whether to take sacred objects from their secret hiding place (maralypi in Warlpiri) as he sets out to look for the woman. This verse may more appropriately occur earlier in the song depending on whether it refers to Honey-Ant's initial search for the woman or to looking for his wife in the ordinary round of domestic life.

47. Nama kila-kila,
    Namaluntu-namaluntuma.

48. Miljalulili kalpinyika,
    Mawinjalili.

49. Mawinja, tajatupatu,
    Kirrinpingi, tajatupatu.

50. Mangkawurru manin-manin
    Tangkawu-tangkawu.

51. Tijantawirri, tawirrilima,
    Najitala tawirrilima.

The singer explained verse 51 as referring to the woman having left her own country (a place called Yulumu) and settling in her husband's country.

52. Mayawurrnga, mirrkilinti,
    Manimaya, mirrkulinti.

53. Mayapa yurrku,
    Lanupayanu mangkinja larrikirri

54. Kujapara jukujuku,
    Ratilanima.

55. Karrana, lututamana,
    Najiti purrkarru-karru.

46. He searched for the sacred place,
    Undecided whether to take the sacred objects.

47. Digging for honey-ants,
    She dug deeply for honey-ants.

48. They embraced lovingly,
    Her thoughts filled with him.

49. Thoughts filled with him, enraptured,
    Ensnared, enraptured.

50. Initiated man
    Has captured her forever.

51. Walked away, sat down,
    I sat down.

52. Wind blew, a hole dug,
    Digging, a hole dug.

53. Watching warily as he worked,
    He went to and from his hole.

54. He looked at his back,
    He looked out from his hole.

55. She walked along, getting a digging stick,
    Sat down to dig.

56. Manakirriri nalpipanalpa,
    Makawirrawi.

57. Nyantawakanata,
    Lanjirrilyirri.

Honey-Ants extract sugar from bush tomato (yawakiyi).

58. Ngwala lanimalani
    Lintima jira.

Honey-ants are captured by digging a hole next to the ant-hole and pushing the ants into the empty hole. The honey-ants are then squashed in a vessel to extract their sweetness. On one level verse 58 depicts an ordinary event, but on another level, in the context of the song as a whole, perhaps it suggests that Honey-Ant was captured by the woman who extracted his sweetness, as much as the woman was captured by Honey-Ant. If this interpretation is correct, two verses later the direction of the symbol is reversed: Honey-Ant asks the woman for honey, but she tells him there is not enough, implying that she now has the honey which Honey-Ant desires (and is denied). The sexual symbolism of honey has its parallel also in Western thought.

59. Jara, wirralintimi,
    Raji wirralintimi.

60. Rrungkala jalpalangka,
    Rrungkala janjilingi.

61. Manakakirri,
    Jilpirliwarra,
    Manyilingili.

As Honey-Ant digs a hole for himself, he discovers that another honey-ant is already there. The significance of verse 61 is that Honey-Ant has many relatives in his own country, unlike the woman who has left her country and kin.

62. Makamarungka
    Lanupayanu,
    Mintirrinjila.

56. She walked unburdened,
    She rested.

57. Bush tomato,
    He sang about it.

58. She extracted the honey
    After Honey-Ant fell into the empty hole.

59. Honey extracted, she returned home,
    Immediately she returned home.

60. He asked for honey,
    Not enough honey.

61. Grass around the ant-holes,
    He threw out stones as he dug,
    Discovering another honey-ant.

62. He searched for another place
    As he went,
    And found one.

63. Mangirrijalatuka
    Lanupayanu,
    Marlikitali.

64. Mangitilyi-tilyi ngirriwangkalyarra
    Winanji ngayutirrpi-tirrpi.

In verse 64 Honey-Ant listens for humans, one of his main predators, before going in search of food.

65. Manamalajala
    Lirrijari-jari
    Lananyapanya.

63. He decorated for a love ceremony
    As he went,
    String crosses like dog ears.

64. Honey-Ant listened
    Before going hunting.

65. At Honey-Ant's hole
    She sat down
    To dig.

Thomas Jangala, 1971

Some Anbarra Songs

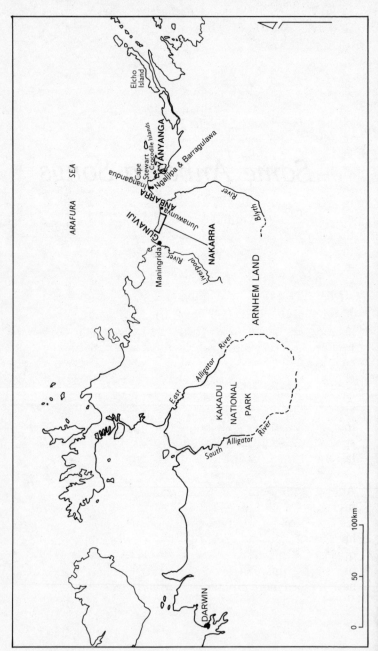

4 The Anbarra and their neighbours

Some Anbarra Songs

The Anbarra or "River Mouth" people live in north-central Arnhem Land in the Northern Territory. Their clan lands and traditional hunting grounds lie on either side of the wide mouth of the Blyth River, some two hundred and fifty kilometres due east of Darwin and about forty kilometres east of the Aboriginal settlement of Maningrida, where some Anbarra now live for at least part of the year. Some clan members prefer to live at outstations on their clan lands, either all the year round or for part of it. The Anbarra speak the Gijingarli dialect of the Burarra language, though many of them are fluent in neighbouring languages such as Nakarra and Gunaviji. Nowadays most Anbarra also speak English as a second language.

Clans in this part of Arnhem Land comprise small groups of Aboriginal people, often closely related, who reckon their group membership through their fathers and together own estates of land. They also believe in, and in a sense "own", a common set of spirit beings whose activities are thought to be closely related to their own lives and well-being. In some cases these spirits are regarded as having been active as creator figures in the distant past, often known as the Dreaming, when the world as humans know it took shape. Other spirits are closely associated with particular locations on clan lands and are often linked mythologically.

Clan songs, known as *manikay* by many Arnhem Land Aborigines, are about these clan spirits or gods, which manifest themselves as animals, plants or manufactured objects as well as spiritual essences. Sometimes these deities have been called totems. The songs celebrate their essential qualities, which may be understood from observing their present-day manifestations as plants or animals but which have a much more profound religious meaning for the owning clans. The songs from Djambidj and Goyulan printed here belong to the *manikay* genre and are spoken in the Gijingarli dialect.

Margaret Clunies Ross

Songs from Djambidj

Djambidj is the name of one song series belonging to a group of Anbarra clans. There are many other clan songs in the region, each with its unique combination of song subjects. Djambidj comprises twenty-one of these. At each recital singers may choose their own subjects or combination of subjects from the Djambidj repertoire, but they often group their songs in performance according to a "seaways — landways" dichotomy, for such a division of the world comes naturally to a coastal people. For example, a singer may begin a performance with several verses of the Shark song, followed by several from Monsoon and Black Bittern. Then he might move to a selection of songs from his landways repertoire, choosing Cockatoo, Marsupial Mouse and Boomerang.

Djambidj may be performed in ritual contexts, especially at funerals, or as entertainment after dinner in the evening when family groups are relaxing after a day out hunting or gathering food. Among the Anbarra, only men sing clan songs, though both men and women own them. A few men in each generation become recognised clan song singers and they emerge as public performers usually when they are in their forties. However, they have practised and listened to their songs constantly since childhood.

These performers are real specialists. First they have to keep in mind all the customary song words and melodic phrases appropriate to between twenty and thirty song subjects. Then they must be able to perform them, often for long periods, improvising their choice of customary phrases, rather like a jazz singer does, in short verses of set structure. The language of these songs is distinct from Burarra in vocabulary and grammar. Another skill the singer has to master is the creation of a continuous but variable rhythm for each subject, which he beats out on a pair of hardwood clapsticks. He also has to work cooperatively with a didjeridu player, who provides him with a steady drone on his pipe plus a series of rhythmic hoots on the overtone. In some situations these singers may also be directing a group of dancers.

The songs that follow are single verses from six Djambidj subjects, recorded between 1975 and 1982.

Ngalalak

Wang-gurnga guya, wang-gurnga guya, gulob'arraja,
  ngwar-ngwar larrya, maningala rarey Ngaljipa.
Jamburr bujarinya, blayriber larrya, garrarra-garrarra,
Ngwar-ngwar larrya, blayriber larrya, jamburr bujarinya,
  Ngaljipa guya, garambak mbana.
Yeliliba guya, ngwar-ngwar larrya, garrarra-garrarra,
  rarrchnga guya, blayriber larrya.
Ga-garrarra rarrchnga guya.
Ngaljipa guya, ngwar-ngwar worrya, jamburr bujarinya,
  blayriber larrya, ngwar-ngwar worrya, maningala rarey,
  rarrchnga guya, Gulgulnga guya.
Ngwar-ngwar worrya, yirpelaynbelayn, rarrchnga guya
  Ngaljipa guya.
Ngwayrk, ngwayrk, Gulgulngam.

There is often a mythological connection between the song subjects of a given series, as there is in Djambidj, for example, between White Cockatoo, Wild Honey and Hollow Log and Crow. The cockatoo song mentions the names of two wells at places called Ngaljipa and Barragulawa where cockatoo lives. Cockatoo and a spirit didjeridu named Mangabupija created Barragulawa. There in the upland eucalypt forest cockatoo and other totems such as crow and hollow log gather to sing and dance Djambidj. Cockatoo plays Mangabupija while crow sings and plays clapsticks.

White Cockatoo

White cockatoo, white cockatoo gorging on grass seeds,
  dancing and leaping in the sky
    at Ngaljipa.
At his upland forest home he eats corms and dry grass
  seeds,
    his crest bobbing up and down.
He dances and leaps, greedy for grass seeds at his forest
  home, at Ngaljipa where he plays didjeridu.
See him leap, his crest rising and falling, see him eat
  rarrcha grass and corms!
See his crest bob up and down as he eats the *rarrcha* grass!
At Ngaljipa he dances, his crest bobbing, gorges and
  belches, dances again and leaps, eats *rarrcha*
    at his birthplace Gulgulnga;
See him dance in the sky, see him eat *rarrcha* grass at
  Ngaljipa!
He calls *ngwayrk ngwayrk* at Gulgulnga.

Frank Malkorda, 1978

Wama–Dupun

'Nga miwarl mbena, gungupa yoryordeya, nakurra
   wargolgolya,
      barlbag-barlbag merney, biyorda ngurrmuryala, Garlnga
      miwarl yana.
Wurrjalab' lambirney, kolupanda yayey, Badurra yibirri-
   ibirr.
      a la la la la
Jarpa murrayala.
Gungupa yordey-yorda, damerra wurrjalaba, a
   barlbag-barlbag merney, damerra wurrjalaba, kolupanda
   yibirri yibirr, Badurra yibirriyibam.

*This song is about two spirit beings, wild honey and hollow tree, the one living
inside the other, reflecting the fact that wild bees often make their nests inside
hollow tree branches. Honey is a prized food among Aborigines, and is therefore
associated with life and prosperity. Hollow trees, on the other hand, are as
much connected with death as with life, and, in particular, with mortuary
ceremonies. People prepare ossuaries from large hollow logs and paint them
with clan emblems of the dead whose bones lie inside them. Two coffin-types are
appropriate to Djambidj owners, namely Dupun and Badurra.*

Wild Honey and Hollow Tree

Spirit women belonging to wild honey hang up their
   baskets at Garlnga, full of fat sugar bag, cut, waxy cells
     oozing dark, viscous honey.
Hollow tree, Wurrjalaba, Badurra hollow log coffin, dry
   wood,
Full of fat sugar bag, gathered by spirit women at Garlnga,
   dark honey —
     a la la la la
Wild honey seeps and stains the dry tree trunk —
Fat sugar bag, oozing with dark, viscous honey, hot stuff,
oozing from dry wood, from Badurra hollow log coffin.

                      Frank Gurrmanamana, 1975

Muralkarra

Daunyiley-nyiley, gaya barrnga, gulbi birrirra warralanga,
  wardupalma, birrirra borja, Wakwakwak, jirnbangaya.
Birrirra borja, garma borja, Garanyula-nyula, Warduba
  jirnbanga.
Birrirra borja, wandalanga, gurta birrirala.
  wak wak wak
Bianga borja, jirnbanga.
Badurra borja, wandalanga, a Maraychnga, daunyiley-
  nyiley,
    Badurra Wardupalmam.

*Crow is a creature who is intensely curious about everything to do with funerals
and so, as befits their elaborate ceremonial, he is a skilled dancer and musician.
He perches on hollow log coffin, called here by two names, Badurra and
Maraych, just as, in fact, Djambidj owners have crow painted at the top of their
ossuaries. He lives in the upland forest and can be heard rubbing firesticks
together. Their sound becomes his cackling laugh and the sticks themselves
seem to be transformed into clapsticks.*

*Crow and hollow log coffin also have a celestial existence, for they are
believed to form a constellation of stars in which hollow log is surrounded by a
flock of dancing crows. Crow's heavenly track must be at a particular point
above the horizon in the early morning, looking east from the Blyth River, at
the climax of the final disposal of the bones of dead Djambidj clanspeople.*

Crow

Crow plays and sings, rubs his firesticks together – see his
    track in the skies! – gets up to dance and tap
    his sticks – Wakwak's a dancing man.
Crow taps his sticks, perches on hollow log, dances at
    Garanyula, his camp in the upland forest –
        Wardupalma's his clan.
He climbs on Badurra – see his heavenly track! he's
    dancing up above.
    wak wak wak
A flock of crows caw to each other as they eat, then rise
    to dance.
Crow perches on Badurra – see his heavenly track! – on
    Maraych; he plays and sings, Wardupalma clansman
    dancing on Badurra.

Frank Malkorda, 1982

Dalwurra

Dalwurrayey, gurray jarrjarr, baney jarrey, wogarl ngurrey,
    naduduba.
Milja baymirra ganurayey, burgunja gama, gajurdayey,
    milja baymirra ganurada.
Werlyadaba, warnaramba, gurray jarrjarrba, Nganda-
    ngandandey.
Gama burgunja, ganurayey, bulogar leybayey,
    guley guley
Gajurdayey werlwerlraja.
Milja baymirra ganurayey, Nganda-nganda, berlga
    wunaramba, Gurraybabam.

*Bittern inhabits the shoreline and sand dunes of the Arnhem Land coast and so
is especially associated with estates of Djambidj-owning clans that border the
Arafura Sea. Two of these are Junawunya by the mouth of the Blyth River and
Inangandua (called* Nganda-nganda *in the song) further to the east on Cape
Stewart.*

Black Bittern

Bittern walks the beaches and tidal creeks
  always in search of fish,
  he's still, moving his head from side to side,
Then flies off, alights and walks the beach
  after the receding tide, head always moving.
A flock rises up and flies away
  from the dark, glossy-leaved *warnaramba* bushes,
  from the beach
    home to Inangandua.
Bittern flies off from the beach head, from the white dunes,
  guley guley,
Alights and follows the tide out.
Rises up in a flock, always moving his head, always
  fishing at Inangandua,
  picking his way between the spinifex and the
  warnaramba bushes
  on Gurriba island.

Frank Malkorda, 1982

Barra

Ngawarl-ngawarl-ngawayarl, ngawarl-ngawarl-ngawayarl,
   jamburcha gulabogbog.
Ngawarl-ngawarl-ngawayarl, machicha Gulabogbog,
   gunamba yalariala, jikarna jikarna.
Buyamalar-malar, Watera, gunamba yalariala.
Ngawarl-ngawarl-ngawayarl, Marra poy-poy yaney,
   gundariana.
   la la la la la
Jamburcha Gulabogbog.
Marra poy-poy yaney, gundariana, a jikarna jikarna,
   Gulabogbog,
   ngawarl-ngawarl, Nganda buypuyanam.

*Barra is the name of the north-west monsoon. Every year, to mark the
beginning of the wet season about December, he appears like a fighting man
upon the horizon, clutching a warrior's dilly-bag between his teeth in his rage
and brandishing a curved fighting stick. Barra is also called* Watera *and* Marra
in this song.

Monsoon

Barra stands ready for battle, a whirlwind about to bear
down,
a black cloud on the horizon.
A whirlwind about to bear down, he stands clenching a
fighting bag between his teeth.
From the west he gathers force in mid-ocean, brandishing
his fighting stick.
Watera beings to blow, from the west he gathers force in
mid-ocean,
like a whirlwind Marra stands ready to bear down upon
his track.
la la la la la
Member of the Gulabogbog clan, he stands as a black
cloud.
Marra stands ready to bear down upon his track,
brandishing his curved fighting stick,
whirlwind coming to Inangandua,
he rushes forward.

Frank Gurrmanamana, 1978

Juray

Nyurra-nyarrarra yay, nyurrarra-nyarrarra yay, burdodpa
   dardumja Kamalangga, wayurwayurwa, nokuwar worrya,
   juraya ngana.
Malka rdinya-rdinya gopurwarl mbeneya, rarrkma raba
   Kamalangga.
Burdod-burdod wanarranga laulowa.
Burdodpa darja juraya nganey marlka rdinya-rdinya
   rarrkma rabam.

*Anbarra people associate eel with Barra, the north-west monsoon. Before the
wet season, two eels, who are said to be the sons of Waitbark, the monsoon,
stand up at different points along the Arnhem Land coast and speak to one
another: "Things are no good, there's no wind." With that they both fart and the
small wind created is the signal for the monsoon to begin.*

*The song also refers to a variety of eel types, belonging to different "skins"
(malk) or subsection groups. Some of them belong to named clans, to which
Aborigines also belong, and can be distinguished by their various colours and
markings. The terms used for these patterns may also refer in other contexts to
common elements of Aboriginal design, such as cross-hatching and dotted infill,
which often appear on bark paintings and other, more traditional painted
surfaces.*

Eel

He lies asleep in his lair, asleep underwater, only his throat
  showing,
Under a rock he lies waiting for the wind, farting a little
  "sh sh".
Eel of the Kamalangga clan starts to swim slowly, then
  dances in his lair, at the mouth of his hole.
Bright coloured eels with different skins get together —
  black head and white belly meets striped and spotted
  Kamalangga clansman.
Wanarranga and *laulowa* fish are countrymen to that hard,
  dry-skinned fellow.
He's still waiting for the wind, eel, farting a little "sh sh",
  spotted and striped.

Frank Gurrmanamana, 1978

Songs from Goyulan

Goyulan is another *manikay* song series from north-central Arnhem Land. The name *goyulan* means "morning star". This series is part of a song line that extends both south-east and north-east from the Blyth River region. Morning star is one of its central emblems. The songs recorded here were sung in 1982 by Johnny Mundrugmundrug and Jack Riala and explained to me by Mundrugmundrug at Maningrida in early 1986.

Like Djambidj, Goyulan celebrates a set of spirit-beings in a series of over thirty song subjects. Like Djambidj also, there is a basic division of these subjects into seaways and landways groups. Many of the Goyulan songs, particularly those from the seaways division, refer to places and mythological happenings that are located geographically well to the east of Anbarra territory among the Crocodile Islands and on Elcho Island. Not surprisingly, then, a number of the Goyulan song words have been identified as from Yanyanga (a language spoken by people living among the Crocodile Islands) rather than related to Burarra.

Parrayt-parrayt

Galinba lurowey, galinba lurowey, bunayarlarley.
Kapulumbo ruto, Dikarr wurpurlma, kapulumbo ruto,
  ngurromurro ngakey.
Parrayt-parrayt-parrayt Dikarrwo.
Galinba lurowey, kapulumbo ruto.
Ngurromurro ngako, parrayt-parrayt, galinba lurowey,
  kumleyana, Dikarr wurpurlma, ganjarjar waton.

Parrayt-parrayt or Dikarr is a fish spirit-being of the open sea.
Mundrugmundrug described it as flying like an aeroplane. Whatever its precise
identity, it seems to jump and fly out of the water. As canoe speeds along,
Parrayt-parrayt jumps up in fright before the paddlers.

Parrayt-parrayt

Parrayt-parrayt fishes far out to sea, in middle waters;
Parrayt-parrayt fishes far out to sea, in middle waters.
Dikarr jumps up, leaps above the surface
  in fright –
Canoe has churned the wave.
Parrayt-parrayt, Dikarr
  fishing far out to sea, jumping in fright at canoe,
    fishing in middle waters.

                    Johnny Mundrugmundrug, 1982

Lipa-lipa

Kuloworo ngako, Jurturrunga, kuloworo ngako, Jurturrunga,
  ngaparl-ngaparlyuna,
Ngaparl-ngaparlyuna, karlnga mirring-guley, Jurturrungo.
Mirring-ganganey, Birril-pirrilyaley,
Kurral-korral, karlnga mirring-guley, kuloworo,
Kuloworo ngako, Burlnyiny wurrum,
Ngaparl-ngaparlyuna, karnyitinga, jilauwurra ngako,
  Kurrolwuna, ngakowuna, Burlnyiny, ngaparl-ngaparlyo,
  jilauwurram.

*Lipa-lipa is the name of the dugout canoe, which is believed to have been
introduced to Arnhem Land Aborigines by Macassan traders from South East
Asia. Originally, though, the canoe song was about a bark boat, which came
into being in the Dreamtime. At that time a spirit man named Mukarr made
canoe out of bark and equipped it with paddles and a sail. He set out on a
journey from a place called Mitpwiwili or Burralko in the direction of Elcho
Island to the east of the Blyth River region and travelled westward towards the
Crocodile Islands. There he visited Murungga Island and continued west to
Jurto, the north west Crocodile Island. There canoe encountered rough seas and
towering waves which broke it to pieces.*

Canoe

Canoe broke up at Jurto, canoe smashed to pieces at Jurto,
Canoe visited Elcho and the Crocodile Islands,
And Mukarr came to Birril-pirril,
Mukarr named Kurral-korral and paddled canoe to Elcho,
Canoe came also to Burlnyiny,
  canoe equipped with paddle, travelling to Burlnyiny.

Johnny Mundrugmundrug, 1982

Manikurdorrk

Wurrakan langarito, wurrakan langarito, wurey-urey-ureyo.
Kurrupurlonganey, kapulo watama, dumba wilingo,
   wurey-urey-ureyo.
A wurrakan, wurrakan, kurrpurlongurio, dartun.
Yanjanga, kurrpurlonga, wilwilunga, dartununa, langarito,
   dartun,
   yanjanga, wiliwilingam.

*Brolga spends his time in the freshwater swamps, standing up in the hot sun
and searching for his favourite food, the corm of the spike rush.*

Brolga

Brolga stands up in the hot sun, brolga stands up
  in the hot sun — he flies off looking for food;
In the dry season heat he stands and walks around
  in the billabong, visits the lily places.
Ah brolga, brolga standing in the hot sun, talking in
  language,
  walking in heat, talking brolga talk, standing in the sun,
  talking, walking again in the swamp places.

                                    Jack Riala, 1982

Barranyji

Barranyji, barranyji, Turundoway.
Barranyji, barranyji, Turundo-murrum.
Kapubarringaria, dirrigiu, Gurdawurlowa, wokalama,
  Turundum.
A barranyji, barranyji, ngaywilinga, murngurlinga,
  Turundo-murro, kumbaytmirrey, jalawortawarrio,
rarringwuna,
    Turundom.

Sugar glider, known as barranyji, *lives at Turundoway on Elcho Island, by the red ochre cliffs that lie beside the salt water. Here there is a famous red ochre quarry, where glider has his home and listens to the noise of the waves.*

Sugar Glider

Sugar glider, sugar glider, his country's Turundoway,
Sugar glider, sugar glider, his paws digging at Turundoway,
Listening to the salt sea waves beside red ochre cliffs,
Eating pandanus fruits at his camp Gurdawurlo,
   gliding around Turundoway,
Ah *barranyji, barranyji,* at home on Elcho Island,
Paws digging, tail grasping at Turundoway.

Johnny Mundrugmundrug, 1982

Goyulan

Garkatununa gurrey-gurrey,
Garkatununa dumbal-mirrey,
Garkatununa gurra-gurrey,
Gagalwuro marranyaley,
Kartanuna Bornumbirrey,
Kartan watama gagalwuro,
Goyulan ngaraka karnuro,
Mirlmardanwey ngarakey,
Kuromoto burlpurlwey,
Garkatununa wuloloyoney gagalwurem.

Goyulan or Bornumbirr is the name of morning star, the planet Venus. This important song gives its name to the whole series known as Goyulan and is central to the rom *or* marrajura *ceremony, which Aborigines from this part of Arnhem Land believe to have been instituted in honour of the morning star spirit. During the course of the ritual a long pole, painted and decorated with red ochre and white pipe clay, wrapped with banyan fibre string and entwined with yellow and white and orange feathers, is prepared and carried in an elaborate morning star dance. It represents the essence of the spirit being.*

The song treats Morning Star as a celestial body, a personified female figure and a ritual icon. She appears in the sky every day before dawn and, when dawn breaks, she "dies" or goes away. Her disappearance causes acute grief to a group of spirit people who institute ritual proceedings designed to get her back. This Dreamtime happening is believed to be the origin of the marrajura *rites that Aborigines still practise.*

Morning Star

Morning Star comes and confronts the dawn,
A cluster of morning star
Confronts the dawn,
Coming from red ochre country,
Morning Star, *bornumbirr*.
Morning Star is coming,
True bone, true substance of *bornumbirr*,
Orange and white feathered string
Bound around her body,
Around the morning star pole.

Johnny Mundrugmundrug, 1982

Wangarra

Puwey puwey puwey,
Ngaychiwuna birawangey,
Munyarirrungo rembi-rembey,
Wuymugo warchirrey,
wala-walarama rumchirrey,
Munyarirrungo bularr-pularr,
Ngaychiwuna gurrey-gurreym.

Wangarra, or Spirit Man, together with a host of other spirits, spend their nights singing and dancing Goyulan in honour of Morning Star. They hope by this means to avert her daily death when dawn comes and to entice her back to live with them permanently. In the dance that may accompany this song both men and women dancers mime Spirit Man's grief at Morning Star's departure by hitting their heads in a stylised display of sorrow.

Spirit Man

"Wey, puwey, wey, puwey",
Spirit Man cries, laments for Morning Star,
Dancing to bring her home,
Dances and sings for her all through the night,
Always leading the corroboree.
Spirit Man dances along a defined track,
Cries and mourns for her as he goes.

Johnny Mundrugmundrug, 1982

Some Wangkangurru Songs

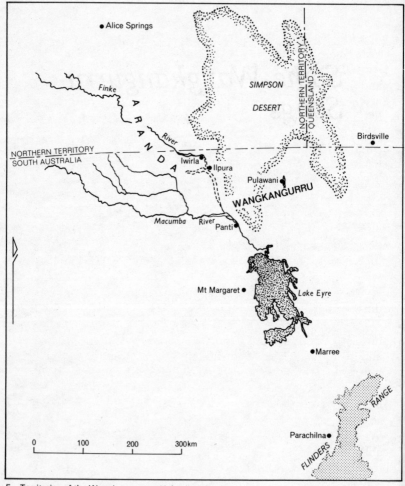

5　Territories of the Wangkangurru and the Aranda

Some Wangkangurru Songs

Wangkangurru oral literature was extensive: it consisted mainly of myths and associated song cycles similar to those described for Aranda, the north-western neighbour of Wangkangurru, by T.G.H. Strehlow in his *Songs of Central Australia*. Knowledge of these traditions was highly esteemed and jealously guarded. The sequence of verses followed the myths and was strictly laid down: anyone caught "frog-hopping", that is, omitting a verse in a sequence, was ridiculed; and in early days such a person could even be in serious trouble. Each verse usually had a "name", that is a key-word by which it was known. This key-word like the other words in a verse was often archaic or in process of disappearing from general use. All words in a verse could be repeated with various modifications and additions. There were however also other types of songs, usually regarded as transient, and described as "rubbish" songs. These dealt with adventures of individuals, such as travel, seeing the first train, or a fight between two old men. These verses also had a "name", but the words were more readily comprehensible in terms of the ordinary language.

Wangkangurru people had begun gradually leaving their home in the Simpson Desert before the turn of the century and by 1901 the last group had left, never to return. They did not forget about their homeland. Even in the nineteen sixties and early seventies there were a few elderly people who had been born in the desert and who could recall the traditional songs and stories that had been handed down among Wangkangurru people for generations. The most knowledgeable of all was the late Mick McLean (Irinjili) and the songs transcribed here are mainly from him.

In the course of his recitals Mick McLean would occasionally make explanatory comments. These comments, enclosed in brackets, are alongside the verse. When spoken in

Wangkangurru a translation has also been given. Comments, in italics, regarding the style of singing are clearly mine.

Luise A. Hercus

Kati-Thanda, Lake Eyre

Of the songs connected with particular features of the landscape, those dealing with Lake Eyre are amongst the most striking. Lake Eyre or Kati-Thanda was south of the country of the Desert Wangkangurru, but it lay in the path of their travels to get red ochre from near Parachilna in the Flinders Ranges. An old man called Tjangili went on an ochre expedition with a group of men from the central Simpson Desert in about 1880. On his return he made a song about Kati-Thanda which Mick McLean learnt from him. Being "made up" within the living memory of the last speakers this song came into the category of "rubbish" songs.

Tjangili's Song

Kati-Thandá wardáyi   yadéyi ya Kati-Thandá
Wamará wamará pantjinánga téyi ya   Kati-Thandá
Wardéyi wardéyi   ya Kati-Thandá yalá.

The Heat Song

Warritharú   yiltayiltá warritharú
Yiltayiltá wamarú   tjiká
Panturúlu ná.

This was a more traditional verse about Lake Eyre. It was said that by singing it repeatedly one could cause a terrible heat-wave. The last person who could sing it was the late Maudie Naylon of Birdsville, who sang it in 1971.

Tjangili's Song

Kati-Thanda is yonder, not too far, Kati-Thanda
The winds endlessly circle over Kati-Thanda
Yonder, not too far, is Kati-Thanda

Mick McLean, 1970

The Heat Song

From afar it comes up, from afar
It comes up, the searing wind
From the great salt lake.

Maudie Naylon, 1971

The Spirit Song about Lake Eyre

1. Wintí tjilpánai wintí tjilpánai
   Ya pílpapílpaténte ya pílpapílpaténte
   Wintí tjilpánai wintí tjilpaténte

2. Wintínje pilpanéle
   Wintínje pilpané
   Warpínjelénje
   Warpínjelerínje
   Wintínje pí

3. Wintínje pilpanélaya
   Wintínje pílpanéleye
   Warpínjelérinjé

An old Wangkangurru man was one of the many who went to the Killalpaninna Mission on the lower Cooper late last century after leaving the desert. He claimed that one night a spirit had led him all over the Lake Eyre country and had given him songs. He handed these on to his young relatives Jimmy Russell (Wanga-mirri, "Many Mornings") and Leslie Russell (Wanga-pula, "Two Mornings") who recorded them at Marree in 1968. These songs are semi-traditional.

Winti Pilpa *refers to the Warrana, the mythical being who travels over Lake Eyre: his body is the whirlwind and only his eyebrows are showing. All the dingoes in the vicinity of the lake belong to him, and woe betide anyone who touches them.*

The Spirit Song about Lake Eyre

1. "Only Eyebrows" he is called,
   He is only eyebrows.
   "Only Eyebrows" he is called,

2. "Only Eyebrows",
   "Only Eyebrows",
   He travels crossway, across the lake,
   Crossways indeed
   "Only . . .

3. "Only Eyebrows",
   "Only Eyebrows",
   He travels crossways across the lake.

4. Piyáyatjána piyáya tjánanjée
   Yúriyúrî márdanjée
   Yáya yúriyúri má . . .

5. Welénje málka yáya welénje málka njái
   Kurdánje kárilínje

6. Malkénje málka njéye malkénje málka njé
   Yurínje málka njé

7. Yerére pingkénje thiwíle
   Palkénje thiwenjé pi
   Palkénje thiwenjé
   Pingkénje thiwíle
   Waríwu parenjé
   Kakénje lé

8. Warénje parenjée
   Kakénje lélinjéye
   Palkénje thiwenjé
   Pingkénje thiwí

The piyatja goblins live on the slopes of Mt Margaret, on the west side of the lake.

4. The *piyatja* goblins, the *piyatja* goblins are painted up
   Like banded snakes they look,
   Yes, like banded snakes.

5. They are dancing now, painted up
   You see them sleeping by the creek.

6. They are painted, all painted,
   Like banded snakes they are painted.

7. They resemble dark flowers
   Flowers in the distance by the lake
   Flowers in the distance by the lake
   Dark flowers
   In the distance the huge flock
   Of crows.

8. In the distance the huge flock
   The flock of crows
   Flowers in the distance by the lake
   Dark flowers.

Jimmy and Leslie Russell, 1968

The Seed Song from Pulawani

The myth and song particularly associated with the *mikiri* well at *Pulawani* in the central Simpson Desert was one particularly close to Mick McLean, it was the song that belonged above all to his sister Topsy *(Ikiwiljika* "Cleaning Seed") who was born near there. When Topsy died in 1974 he sang the song for her and added sorrowfully: "When I die, there will be nobody to sing my song, *Pirlakaya.*" The *Pulawani* song deals with the drama of drought and rain in one of the most inhospitable areas on earth, and it was sung with emotion and intensity. It was the main song used for the increase in *ngarralja*, that is hard seed, such as acacia and pigface seed. In the increase ceremonies special round stones were placed at the butt of trees and the relevant verses sung. These round stones were a most precious commodity in this vast area of sanddunes, where there was no local stone apart from gypsum.

The Seed Song from Pulawani

A description of the searing heat and desperate drought in the Simpson Desert.

1. Thrukú thurkungáya
   Thrukú thurkungáya ralíyariljái

This verse is sung in a whisper, repeated five times, it is a spell to turn what is dry green.

2. Ngárditjíta kúdna-kúdna
   Ngárditjíta kúdna-kúdna

3. Ngárditjíta ngáljurúka
   Ngárditjíta ngáljurúka

The old dead stump begins to become green now:

4. Ngárditjífa kúdnandríta
   Ngárditjífa kúdnandrí

New leaves are beginning to show and roots are growing:

5. Thakáta wírthiwírthi ya
   Thakáta wírthi ya
   Thakáta malurúka malurú

6. Thákántatjé yáta
   Thakántatjé yáta
   Thákawíritje

7. Thakárata tálpalunté yata
   Thakárata tálpalunté ya
   Thakárata malurúka malurú

The Seed Song from Pulawani

1. Dry leaves everywhere,
   Dry leaves fallen on the ground.

2. Dry stump, become light green!
   Dry stump, become light green!

3. Dry stumps grow green!
   Dry stumps grow green!

4. Dry stumps, dry stumps becoming soft green.
   Dry stumps, dry stumps becoming soft green.

5. Roots are growing
   Roots are growing
   Roots are swelling with sap.

6. Roots are running out further
   Roots are running out further
   Roots are growing.

7. Roots are spreading further.
   Roots are spreading further
   Roots are swelling with sap.

8. Athathálpinté máthathalpinté
   Lintinjára wirúdnité njéntinjáya wirúru

9. Kuná kuná katayáltu
   Pákatayáltu
   Panjí thirrá

10. Purrkiljá yáyá kuná kuná purrkiljá yáyá
    Kuná katayáltu pá katayáltu

11. Kúdnungkulúntani tjálpanái
    Yangkúdnungkulúntani tjálpanái
    Yángkwáka
    Apatalá waratjálpanái

(kadnha kardatjiringa nhamparda)

12. Yángkwídnjndu líntani tjálpanái
    Yángkúdnungku luntani tjálpanái
    Yángkawálpita wárái

Those seeds are all ready now!

13. Parríyé mantá, yántaráya palthíye mantá
    Palthíye nguthá

(uta nhukulu karinha tharnira-lk' arniri.)

14. Kalpítá yálawíriká
    Kalpítá yálawíriká
    Yá pakákúra yálanádnai
    Yá pakákúra yálanádnai

This particular verse is in Aranda although it belongs to Wangkangurru country.

8. The roots are growing big, huge,
   Tall trees are standing there.

9. Green, green colour all around
   Green plants in vast numbers
   Are standing up straight.

10. Ripening plants with green colour all around
    Green colour all around.

11. They put it by the tree.
    Yes, they put it by the tree.
    The stone
    They put a stone at the side of the tree.

(They bury a stone at the butt of a tree.)

12. The stone is by the tree,
    Yes, the stone is put by the tree,
    The stone is at the side.

13. They take the seed, with a stone they pound it.
    They pound it, they smash it.

(Now tomorrow we will eat them)

14. They grind the seed.
    They grind the seed.
    May that tree remain there, standing alone.
    May that tree remain there, standing alone.

15. Línthapátarálaná
    Wiljanarí
    Yalanái wiljarái

16. Lákalumpá kalumpá
    Língirpengé wiljulánaradná ya'ra

17. Málkérawáki kirárawárá mpalára wára
    Málkérawáki kirárawárá
    Ampalaralára

Mick McLean said that this verse was "right alongside my country", it referred to the Pulawani *well itself, and to the ceremony which was to be held right there.*

18. Márlilta máarliltá
    Márlilta máarliltá
    Lápatankáarinja
    Lápata wánpirénjalú

The large pounding slab, ngampa, *used for cracking hard seed, is here being likened to a stone axe, and it is referred to by the Aranda term for stone axe in the following verses.*

19. Lapatánkadnhá líntadnjí
    Tjudnúru wátaye yáya
    Lapatánkadnhá líntadnjí

20. Ngalkálkatíntja
    Kuméluméla ngalí
    Thapatalíntja kuméluméla
    Thapatalíntja ngalí

15. It stands there
    A dark tree,
    A dark tree alone.

16. Clover is growing there, clover.
    They start cooking the dough.

17. They are painting themselves for a ceremony.
    They are painting-up
    For a ceremony.

18. The handle,
    The handle,
    It is a stone-axe he looks at
    It is a stone-axe he holds.

19. It is a stone axe, a stone
    He looks at it, he picks it up,
    It is a stone-axe, a stone.

20. They are pounding,
    They are smashing up the seeds
    With a stone they are smashing them up
    With a stone.

21. Rúmarná tjukwáwa yáayayée
    Yá rumarná tjukwa waráwarái
    Yá rumarná tjukulpirú
    Yá rumarná tjukulpirú pirái

(Pulawani is in my country, a hundred miles east of Ilpura on the Finke River. That is the end of the story.)

21. They are breaking off the shell from the seeds to
        make food
    They are breaking it off to the side
    They are breaking and tossing away the shell.

                                        Mick McLean, 1968

Carpet Snakes

There are long lines of song dealing with the travels of ancestral Snakes across the desert. They camp at a number of important sites and encounter many different creatures. One pair of Snakes travel from the Pulawani well to Iwirla waterhole on the Finke River and then to the main Snake site at Panti on the lower Macumba River. They are called ancestral Carpet Snakes but they can change their shape and are really Rainbow Serpents. Just a few extracts from the long song cycle are given here: the translator is guilty of much "frog-hopping". The verses come from recordings made by Mick McLean in 1972.

The huge female Snake *Muntuljuru* is regarded as grotesque and some of the verses connected with her are sung amid much laughter. At one stage, when approaching the Macumba from the sand-hills, she became separated from the male Snake and travelled on alone. We start the extracts from there.

Carpet Snakes

This verse is sung slowly, as the Snake-woman travels determinedly on-wards:

1. Kantí witjatálkáyál-puruká
   Yáriwé weláne
   Yá kantí witjatálkáyál-puruká
   Yáriwé welá

Down in the swale she saw some shell parrots and she sang:

2. Patatharí wírupá
   Tjalpará líndumá
   Wírupá waráyan
   Patatharí wírupá

This verse is then "turned round":

3. Patatharí unpátathará
   Líndamá wirupá waráyan

The male Snake tried to follow her tracks, but failed. He sang:

4. Warpangá wárampangá warpangá
   Yá ngunurá
   Ya ngúnjané réyá

This verse too is then turned round:

5. Ngúnjané réyá
   Ya ngunuráya ya ngúnjanéré
   Warpangá warpangá

Carpet Snakes

1. Like a large waddy, slithering down one sand-hill
   She crosses over to the next.
   Yes, like a large waddy slithering down one sand-hill
   She crosses over to the next.

2. Shell parrots, I hear them
   They are sitting in a tree.
   I can hear them over there,
   Shell parrots I hear.

3. Shell parrots, shell parrots
   Sitting down, I can hear them over there.

4. The wind has covered them over, the wind.
   They have faded,
   Disappeared.

5. They have faded
   Yes disappeared, yes disappeared.
   The wind, the wind!

In the meantime the female saw two mura-mura *women (plump and dwarf-like mythological beings.) She turned herself into a little* yuri-yuri, *a banded snake. One of the two women says, "Sister, that is a little banded snake lying here. It's ours!" And she sang:*

6. Malká rurpená rúrpéyéné, mintenhá
   Yá malká rurpená rurpéyéné, mintenhá!

The Rainbow Serpent Muntuljuru *could see the* mura-mura *people in the distant camp and sang:*

7. Mará piparlá
   Mará purnkunkú
   Líntínthi tjará

The two little women came forward to kill Muntuljuru *with their yamstick, but she turned back to her original size as a huge and brightly-banded Rainbow Serpent. She swallowed the yamstick and the women, too. She then followed the many tracks that led to the* mura-mura *camp. She went there and danced. The* mura-mura *people: men, women and children came and stood in a circle to watch. Here the recitation half turns to song:*

8. Nhúrkaruká, malka ngúru, malka ngúru!

She swallowed them, she swallowed every single thing in the surrounds down to faeces and urine, she even devoured sticks and grinding dishes. But one powerful female mura-mura *witchdoctor had turned herself into a small round pounding stone. She sang:*

9. Mithítjíla larámpurunjéna
   Nhámpuru nhámpurunjé
   Yétéla nhámpuru nhámpurunjé

Most of the words in this verse are said to be "just song". They have no meaning in Wangkangurra, and so cannot be translated into English.

10. Larámpurunjéna
    Nhámpuru nhámpurunjé
    Yétéla   nhámpuru nhámpurunjé

6. The stripes are like ochre rubbed on, just look!
   Yes, the stripes are like ochre rubbed on, just look!

7. I see many,
   I see a lot,
   I am just lying here.

8. She swallowed them, not one, not a single one
   remained!

9. I am a little round stone
   Nhámpuru nhámpurunjé
   Yétéla nhámpuru nhámpurunjé

10. I am a round stone
    Nhámpuru nhámpurunjé
    Yétéla nhámpuru nhámpurunjé

The Rainbow Serpent could not make out who was talking. The little stone sang again several times, turning around the words larampuru njampuru njampuru. *The verse was altered further as follows:*

11. Njampúyura kámpunjampé néndanhána
    Ladámpu njámpu nja ladámpu yampé néndanhá

The Serpent looked round again and so the little stone stopped singing and just made a grunting sound mmmmm.
As the Serpent was leaving she heard the grunting sound. She said: "How could it have happened that I have missed one?" She sang to herself:

12. Wardiké tja wárdiká,
    Wantjá ya warantjá wará ya.

She pretended to leave right away and then came back again. The little stone was still uttering the same verse and making a grunting sound:

13. Njampúyura kámpunjampé néndanhána
    Ladámpu njámpu nja ladámpu yampé néndanhá

The Serpent sang in slow tones, protracting some syllables to a great length:

14. Puranjé wáaranje waranjé yendé parúyulani
    Yendé parúyulané ya wáaranje waranjé

The little stone was still making a grunting sound mmmm. *The Serpent climbed to the top of the sand-hill and looked around. She didn't realise the little stone could talk. So she pretended to leave altogether.*

11. *Njampúyura kámpunjampé néndanhána*
    Ladámpu njámpu nja ladámpu yampé néndanhá

12. That thing, that thing
    Where is it, who is it, who?

13. *Njampúyura kámpunjampé néndanhána*
    Ladámpu njámpu nja ladámpu yampé néndanhá

14. Away in the corner who, who keeps on talking?
    That constant talking who is it, who?

A little way off she saw a flat black beetle of the type known as warranji-warranji. *This beetle is a friend of all carpet snakes and shares their burrows. The Serpent sang:*

15. Wárranji warranjé
    Ya wárranjé warranjé
    Yéye télpalúyuyurláni
    Yéye télparúyuyurlané

16. Yéye télparúyuyurláni
    Yéye télparúyuyurlané télparúyurláni
    Ya wárranji warranjé
    Ya wáranjé warranjé

She made the beetle turn back and go into the camp ahead of her. That is how she caught the little stone and she swallowed it, as it was still grunting mmmm.

That little stone, still going mmmm, *turned into the heart of the Serpent. So all snakes now have a little round heart.*

There was absolutely nothing left in the mura-mura *camp, and so the Serpent* Muntuljuru *left the place, crawling very slowly and laboriously, and singing equally slowly:*

17. Lurnáritjurnéi yéné tjirkilantaná
    Lurnárijurnéi yéné tjirkilantaná
    Lurpénturpéntéréyé

The Serpent had eaten too much and began to feel ill, she could barely move. She crawled into a hole and lay there.

The male Snake was travelling about nearby in the country called Wakarla-warranha, *"Crows Dancing". He sang using mainly Aranda words:*

18. Wakara ridnemáatitjéle meránkapará
    Ya wakara ridnemáatitjéle meránkapará

15. The beetle
    The beetle
    Yéye télpalúyuyurláni
    Yéye télparúyuyurlané

16. *Yéye télparúyuyurláni*
    Yéye télparúyuyurlané télparúyurláni
    Yes, the beetle
    Yes the beetle.

17. Rustling along over prickles,
    Rustling along over prickles,
    Rustling along.

18. At *Wakarla-warranha* I shall stay,
    Yes, at *Wakarla-warranha* I shall stay.

and altering it slightly

19. Arditjé lé perángkapalá
    Ya wakárla riné máatitjéle meránkapará

The male Snake was still looking for his wife. He found the many little tracks leading to the now empty mura-mura camp. He still could not see Muntuljuru's track, but he saw the loose soil by the hole and then he could smell who was in there.

He strangled her there and then because of an earlier incident. He regretted this immediately and dragged the huge limp body out of the hole.

20. Kiwatjá mintjé thiyé míntjepardá mintjereyé
    Míntjakamparí kámparí mené tjeré míntjakamparí
        kámparí
    Míntjepardá mintjéreyé

He tried all kinds of healing herbs on her:

21. Yánthanhá yupilingkú pithé
    Yánthanhá yupelengkú pilé
    Yáthanhá yalpurupá puré

22. Yálpuru pálpuré
    Yáthanhá yalpurupá puré
    Yáthanhá yupelengkú pilé

He went further and further looking for medicinal plants and there are verses for each one of his attempts. The various birds that he encountered he consulted about what to do. Where oh where could he find the right herb?

There was nothing.

19. There I shall stay,
    Yes, at *Wakarla-warranha* I shall stay.

20. He has brought her out to make her come alive.
    To make her come alive he touches her on the top of
       the head
    He has brought her out.

21. Close by he rubs a tree
    Close by he rubs another
    Close by he tries them out.

22. He tries them out,
    Close by he tries
    Close by he rubs.

He decided to bury her, so he had to dig an enormous tunnel. As he dug he sang:

23. Ngírtjardá ngayálarái
    Ngírtjardá ngayálarái
    Ngírtjardá njampíleré
    Ngayálarái
    Ngírtjardá njampíleré

He repeated this verse many times as he dug.

He had a last desperate look over the sand-hills, where could he find the right herb, the right herb to make a healing smoke? He called again to the birds:

24. Paya kípakipá páya nhayáki

And then he saw it, on a sand-hill to the north, the wakimpa *plant [a now probably extinct leguminous plant] and he sang:*

25. Lawára yatanárná yawárdá
    Yálawadnái yála wakímpakimpáya

He picked the plant saying "Here it is at last!" and singing the wakimpa, *verse again. He got ready a big fire for a smoke, he put in the herb and brought* Muntuljuru *back to life. The two great Snakes set off together.*

The following verses describe the Snakes crossing the last big area of sand before reaching Panti.

26. Yanmé tatjí yandé yanmái tatí
    Yandáya tiltjé wadnái tatjí yandá yamá

27. Waráwarí yandí yandáya wará yandá
    Tiltjété wará warí yandáya

23. A hole, a dark tunnel
    A hole, a dark tunnel
    A hole for burying her
    A dark tunnel
    A hole for burying her!

24. Birds! Birds right here!

25. There it stands the very one!
    Close, close indeed the *wakimpa*, the *wakimpa!*

26. They push up small ridges of sand.
    Twisting around, they push up small ridges of sand.

27. From side to side they push up ridges of sand
    Twisting around, they push sand to the side.

They saw the great site at Panti *in the distance, the site that had drawn them from hundreds of miles away, and they sang:*

28. Pántinhá yurrkú watái
    Ya Pántinhá yurrkú watái
    Yá Pántinhá midlá purrthái

The two Snakes hurried down from the sand-hill, they hit the sand with their back, they hit it!

29. Tiráya matjáya karáya rúyu pidní
    Tjarlpáya tarí yandáya tjarlpáya tarí

30. Idná lakúruká ya nambára wáyéye
    Téna lakúruká yanbála wéye dená

There is a small swamp there, with some box-trees. The two Snakes stayed there.

31. Yurántjúu rantjúu yú ridé
    Tjantáaya rayáka
    Yurantjúre tantayá larántju
    Yeliré pantáaya lárá

They came to the creek and found there was a different kind of sand, creek-sand, it was like quicksand!

32. Malpá tharálintá
    Yalarálaa karínhé
    Lá malpá tharálintá.

28. *Panti*! The necks of snakes are held high
    Yes *Panti*! The necks of snakes are held high
    Yes *Panti*! There is that which is prominent.

29. The two of them come out into the flat, they hit the flat
    ground.
    They make ridges of sand between the trees.

30. They are walking along the flat.
    Along the flat they move.

31. The two look this way
    There is water.
    This way
    There is water.

32. There is quicksand!
    Close by, look!
    There is quicksand!

The place was already occupied by another pair of Snakes, so there was a great fight, male against male, female against female.

The song for the fight between the two male Snakes is as follows:

33. Marrpánti marrpantí tíngkwa marrpánti
    Itingkwá marílje mariljé tíngkwa marrpánti

The verse belongs to the plain called Palparra *"Cleared Ground" very close to* Panti, *(i.e., the dancing ground associated with the* Panti *ritual centre). In the History time (meaning Dreamtime to the* Wangkangurru*) the ground was cleared and flattened by the two male Snake-ancestors fighting, rolling round and smoothing the ground like two giant steamrollers. The travelling Snake defeated the other.*

The two Snake women then reared up to fight:

34. Múlulúrtanpá múlulúrthanpé
    Yáa párraká múlulúrthanpá múlulúrthanpái
    Yáa párraká múlulúrthanpá múlulúrthanpái

Muntuljuru *threw the other female over a bank.*

Then all the Snakes approached the great site at Panti. *They sang:*

35. PáRatji ngardáka
    Pántinha mídlapurthára
    Pántinha mídlapurthára
    Ya tínha mídlapurthára
    PáRatji ngardáka
    Pántinha yurrkú watá.

33. They are centipedes, the way they roll round,
       centipedes
    On the flat ground among the pigweed, centipedes!

34. Backbone against backbone,
    Yes over the bank goes a backbone, a backbone,
    Yes over the bank goes a backbone, a backbone.

35. A great flame was burning,
    Panti the prominent one,
    Panti the prominent one,
    The prominent one.
    A great flame was burning,
    Panti! The necks of snakes are held high.

Mick McLean, 1970

Notes

Some Dyirbal Songs

"Dyirbal song types: a preliminary report" by R.M.W. Dixon (pp.206-27 in *Problems and solutions: occasional essays in musicology presented to Alice M. Moyle*, J. Kassler and J. Stubington, eds. Sydney: Hale and Iremonger, 1984) describes the metrical patterns, grammatical and lexical characteristics, and functions of the various song styles. A full account of Dyirbal grammar, with an introductory chapter on the cultural background, is in Dixon's *The Dyirbal language of North Queensland* (Cambridge: Cambridge University Press, 1972). There is an accessible account of Dixon's fieldwork, including how many of the songs came to be recorded, in his *Searching for Aboriginal languages: memoirs of a field worker* (St Lucia: University of Queensland Press, 1983; University of Chicago Press, 1989).

Grace Koch has made a musicology analysis of four different performances of a Gama-style song in her "Dyirbal Gama songs of Cape York" (pp. 43-62 in *Songs of Aboriginal Australia*, M. Clunies Ross, T. Donaldson and S.A. Wild eds, *Oceania Monograph* no 32 University of Sydney, 1987). The only other published account of Dyirbal songs is in *Games, sports and amusements* by W.E. Roth *(North Queensland Ethnography*, Bulletin no 4 Brisbane: 1902.)

R.M.W. Dixon wishes to acknowledge the tremendous help he had in transcribing and translating the songs included here, from the singers themselves; and also from Bessie Jerry, Ida Henry and Andy Denham.

A Central Australian Men's Love Song

The classic ethnography of the Warlpiri (or Walbiri) is *Desert people: a study of the Walbiri Aborigines of central Australia* by M.J. Meggitt (Sydney: Angus & Robertson, 1962). Meggitt's description of social organisation is still considered authoritative, and his book includes a detailed description of male initiation. N. Munn's *Warlbiri iconography: graphic representation and cultural symbolism in a central Australian society* (Ithaca and London: Cornell University Press, 1973) is a study of Warlpiri visual art and its relationship to ceremonies and the Dreaming.

For central Australia generally, T.G.H. Strehlow's monumental study *Songs of central Australia* (Sydney: Angus & Robertson, 1971) is the most important source on song-poetry and its religious contexts. Richard Moyle's two books, *Songs of the Pintupi: musical life in a central Australian society* (1979) and *Alyawarra music: songs and society in a central Australian community* (1986), both published by the Australian Institute of Aboriginal Studies, are studies of the musical aspects of songs. The ceremonial life of women in central Australia is the subject of Diane Bell's book *Daughters of the Dreaming* (Melbourne: McPhee Gribble/Allen and Unwin, 1983).

Some Anbarra Songs

The first recording and translation of Anbarra songs appeared in L.R. and Betty Hiatt's *Songs of Arnhem Land* (Canberra: Australian Institute of Aboriginal Studies, 1966). Since then the Institute has issued two longer musical recordings with accompanying books. These are *Djambidj: an Aboriginal song series from northern Australia* (1981-82) edited by B. Butler and S. Wild (record and cassette) and M. Clunies Ross and S. Wild (book) and *Goyulan the Morning Star* (1988). This cassette and companion book of the same title is the work of Johnny Mundrugmundrug and Margaret Clunies Ross.

Many songs from Djambidj and Goyulan may also be heard as the ritual accompaniment to an Anbarra funeral in the film *Waiting for Harry*, directed by Kim McKenzie (Canberra: Australian Institute of Aboriginal Studies, 1980). Hire of the film can be arranged through the National Library in Canberra. The book *Rom. An Aboriginal Ritual of Diplomacy* (ed. S. Wild, Canberra: Australian Institute of Aboriginal Studies, 1986) gives a full account of another Anbarra ceremony in which Djambidj and Goyulan provide a liturgical accompaniment. The book is beautifully illustrated with photographs of bark paintings which two of the singers made to depict the subjects of their songs.

These songs often refer to Anbarra clan lands and the plants and animals that inhabit them. This relationship has been explored by L.R. Hiatt and Rhys Jones in their "Aboriginal Conceptions of the Workings of Nature" (pp.1-22 of *Australian Science in the Making*, edited by R.W. Home, Melbourne: Cambridge University Press, 1988) and again by Rhys Jones in his "Ordering the landscape" (pp.181-209 of *Seeing the First Australians*, edited by I. and T. Donaldson, Sydney, London and Boston: Allen and Unwin, 1985). Betty Meehan's *Shell Bed to Shell Midden* (Canberra: Australian Institute of Aboriginal Studies, 1982) gives a good idea of Anbarra hunting and gathering lifestyles in a contemporary environment, while L.R. Hiatt's *Kinship and Conflict* (Canberra: Australian National

University Press, 1965) explains their social organisation and religious beliefs.

All the Australian Institute of Aboriginal Studies publications are available from the Institute, G.P.O. Box 553, Canberra, A.C.T., Australia 2601.

Some Wangkangurru Songs

Song Techniques

An outstanding description of these techniques of modifying songs has been given by K. Hale, 'Remarks on Creativity in Aboriginal Verse' in *Problems and Solutions, Occasional Essays in Musicology presented to Alice M. Moyle*, J. Kassler and J. Stubington, eds., Sydney, 1984, 254–262.

Simpson Desert Sites

Wangkangurru people had ceased to occupy the Simpson Desert on a permanent basis by 1902: they had been drifting away gradually over many years, mainly to Killalpaninna Mission and to cattle stations, in search of an easier life. There is evidence that older individuals and small groups of older people went back at various times on short ceremonial and nostalgic visits; but people who grew up after 1902 did not know the area at all. This meant that during the last decade there was nobody who could locate even the main *mikiri* 'native wells', nor the most important claypans nor any of the other sites that were celebrated in the traditional songs of Wangkangurru people. As there is no permanent surface water in the Simpson Desert, Wangkangurru people had been entirely dependent on the wells except after rain. The wells tapped small local subterranean water-supplies, usually about 20 feet below the surface. The explorer David Lindsay had been taken by a Wangkangurru guide to visit nine wells in 1886. Using Lindsay's notes and working out the distances that Lindsay had given in camel-time, the South Australian explorer Denis Bartell relocated these major sites, and in 1983 he showed them to Peter Clark and me (see Hercus, L.A. and P. Clark, 1986 'Leaving the Simpson Desert', *Aboriginal History* 9). The *Pulawani* well, called 'Pudlawinna' by Lindsay, is in the vicinity of the huge and desolate salt-lake called Lake Poolowanna. All that remains now of the well is a shallow depression in the ground. Some stone artefacts, a broken spear and an old parrying shield still lie there, half buried in the sand.

The Reverend Reuther

The Reverend Reuther was a missionary at the great Lutheran mission at Kilallpaninna on the lower Cooper for eighteen years from

1888. The Mission attracted people from all over the Lake Eyre Basin, including many Wangkangurru. Reuther took a keen interest in the languages and traditions of the Lake Eyre Basin. Apart from work on translating the Bible into Diyari he wrote, in German, a great work of thirteen volumes, including dictionaries and a vast store of other information. His work was never published in its original form and even now it is only available in a microfiche edition: J.G. Reuther, *The Diari.*, translated by the Rev. P. Scherer. AIAS microfiche no.2. Australian Institute of Aboriginal Studies, Canberra.

Reuther must have heard from Wangkangurru people at the turn of the century at least some of those very same long song cycles that Mick McLean was still able to recite for me between 1965 and 1977. Reuther gives the exact wording of verse 25 of the present Carpet Snake Song in his Vol X: 72, verse XXI, and of verse 33 in his Vol. X: 70, verse XXIV.

Information on Reuther and his work is available in the recent book by Philip Jones and Peter Sutton, *Art and Land,* South Australian Museum, 1986.